Strangling of American Liberty

Dr. David N. Smeltz

Published by His Word of Truth Ministry
ISBN-13: 978-1511612418
ISBN-10: 151161241X

Forward by Dr. Ron Maggard

I have known of Dr. David Smeltz for many years, but only from a distance. Recently I had the opportunity to begin communicating with him in preparation for some ministry that we were planning in Guatemala. He was to come to our remote area in Guatemala to train pastors and leaders. The more I spoke with Dr. Smeltz the more I felt that he could be a real help and blessing to our ministry and our pastors.

The day finally came when I met David and his wife Susan in the Aurora Airport in Guatemala City. The ministry of David and Susan with our people in Guatemala was a real blessing and we are looking forward to their return for more ministries in the future.

The timing of this book could not be better. People everywhere, whether they are church people or not are searching for truths that they can find in this book. Some of these truths, they may not like, but America needs this reality. Dr. Smeltz is writing about things that most have lived through. Then Dr. Smeltz compares these headline happenings with how they affected America and how they have all come together to this crucial point today and are strangling our liberties.

I believe Dr. Smeltz has written this book because of his real burden for souls, and his hope to awaken God's people, especially here in his native land of America. He also has written because God has given him a real understanding for things as they are in light of biblical prophecy. From David's beginnings in ministry with Dr. Jerry Falwell and his work with the Moral Majority cause of its day, it is evident in this book that Dr. Smeltz has his finger on the pulse of America's liberty. We can only pray **that this book is a help to awaken people to the great danger that is upon our nation.**

Ron Maggard
Baptist Evangelism

Forward

Pastor David Chaffin
Ocala Baptist Temple
Ocala, Florida

The first thing that jumped out as I began reading was you acknowledging the great men in the past who gave you a pattern to follow for Spiritual ministering! As well as acknowledging your present friends in the Gospel ministry. This is a tribute to their Spiritual walking with God.

As I began reading, I could immediately see that you had already seen the same things taking place today in our country that you saw in the past and that is the overturning of truth...calling evil good and good evil. It is sad that the Political world and the News media world is *still so wrapped around personal pride and lies* rather than truthful principals.

It is also amazing that our very own Military are asking today the same questions that you and the others asked, "Why are we here?" No clear plan for achieving victory then and now seems to be the motive to the so-called leaders of America.

Although, the Religious, Financial, Political and Military world are ignoring not only God's truth but also the truths of lessons learned in history: there are still God fearing, Patriotic Americans who love God and this country! Your writing this book is an example of this fact!

Sin *is a reproach to God* and yes, all nations shall be turned into hell that forgets Him! You definitely bring this out! Nevertheless, no changes will take place without God's intervention. Israel is an example of this lesson. They were in bondage for 400 years murmuring and complaining. However, when Israel started crying out to God...He sent them a deliverer!

I pray this book will eventually challenge God's people to stop complaining and start praying! All of the things needing to be done that are mentioned in the book are needful. However, without God America can do nothing!

DEDICATION

This year I will be seventy years old and many people over the years have contributed to my education and knowledge. Some of these people have gone home to be with the Lord and are remembered by their students of which I was one. Many of these men are good friends who have held to the faith in fighting the good fight as they serve. They love America.

Dr. Harold Wilmington, Founder of Liberty Bible Institute, Professor and friend

- ❖ Dr. Jerry Falwell, Founder of Thomas Road Baptist Church and College
- ❖ Dr. Marshall Bond, Pastor and good friend
- ❖ Dr. J.O Grooms founder of Treasure Path to Soul Winning and a good friend
- ❖ Dr. John Bonds, Pastor and friend

Pastor Shannon Foote, Grace Baptist Church for the design of the cover for this book and a good friend

Pastor David Chaffin, Ocala Baptist Temple friend and Prayer partner.

Dr. Dennis Ebert, Missionary to Philippines 35 years and good friend

Dr. Ron Maggard, Missionary to Guatemala, Cuba, Haiti for over 30 years and a good friend

Dr. Ron Minton, Missionary to the Ukraine and a good friend

Dr. Dennis Dodson, Pastor Central Baptist Church, Center, Texas

Pastor Vance Catlin, our home church pastor, Harmony Baptist Church, Plant City, Florida

Pastor Dave Peters, Good friend for over 35 years.

To Susan my wife for her consistent love, devotion: to God and me for 45 years. To our children and grandchildren who have prayed for us. Most of all to my Lord and Savior Jesus Christ

❖ **Deceased**

Table of Contents

Introduction

This book is all about our liberty being stolen from us by liberals and people who are hell bent on destroying America. In 1963, I graduated from High School and went directly into the Army. I was only seventeen years old and wanted to get away from home and start a life on my own. Many of my high school chums went off to college and I went to Fort Jackson, SC tank hill for basic training. I had no idea what I was getting into and I found out very quickly I was going to embark on a new way of life. The training was gruesome and after playing football in high school I thank God, I was ready for it. The rougher it was the better I liked it. Thirteen weeks of training had hardened me and I was physical fit and thirty pounds lighter then when I started. The discipline environment was good for me and I realized I had to obey the orders given to me. I did not always like them, but I knew the training was good. I went home for a short leave after basic training and was surprised at the changes that taken place in four months. I went in the service on June 10, 1963 and it was now October. After my leave was up, I headed to Fort Gordon Georgia for my advance training. I had signed up for the "Signal Corp" but I hated it and the classroom was so boring.

On November 22, 1963, President Kennedy was in Texas and assassinated and the military was in turmoil. We had no idea what was going to take place as the base was placed on high alert. The next day they had a muster (Where all the men would gather outside in formation) and they asked for volunteers. I hated what I was doing and I was one of the first to raise my hand. I had volunteered to go infantry and train in guerrilla training. Once again, I had no idea about what I was doing. Many of the men who were coming into the military were draftees and I had enlisted, so all of us who had, joined were consistently being harassed and called lifers. The draftees complained all the time, about serving in the military. We had twelve weeks of training in the advanced infantry techniques. After completion, we awaited our orders of duty assignment. Many were getting orders to Korea, Germany and my orders were for Hawaii. I was excited about going to Hawaii and thought I had a good assignment. I was surprised when I arrived in Hawaii; it was a lot different than I had anticipated. It was hot and the training at times could be difficult as we concentrated on guerrilla tactics. We were in the jungles and then we were on Hilo where the volcano was. We were a mechanized infantry unit, ready to go at the drop of a hat. I had the privilege to serve with the 25th Infantry Division, the Pacific coast finest military division.

While serving in the Pacific I had little communication with the states. I did not watch television, listen to a radio and we did not have the internet. Most of the communication was word of mouth with those who were coming in from the states. A three-day pass was fun, but when you received $78.00 a month that did not go very far. A hamburger in Hawaii in 1964 was about $3.00. Everybody ate at the chow hall and then would catch the base bus into town. Hanging out at the bars, and restaurants and beach were very common. The majority of the enlisted men, would drink cheap wine ($1.00) a bottle. Those who were drafted seem to have it more together then those who enlisted. In 1964, most of the draftees were in the twenties while enlistees were seventeen and up. Now, there were the lifers who had served for many years.

We were hearing about the riots in the streets with Black and white: more Blacks came in to the service and fights would break out in barracks. The southern boys did not like the Blacks and special those who had rank. The Black's would let you know they were in charge and they were always the loudest in the crowd. The Blacks traveled in a group and they would start a fight with a white person because they outnumbered him. Payday was always hectic as everyone would try to go into town and would come back broke. You had to keep your footlocker locked as stealing was always taking place. The gay bars were always full of vets and the transsexual bars had their fill. I had made some friends with local people and spent most of my time with them. I cannot say I did not visit the wrong places. I did because I thought it was funny and sick at the same time. I had grown up in

Miami, Florida and I had not witnessed the sodomites in action. To me a queer was a queer and I did not see anything gay about them. Hotel Street in Honolulu was a wild place and you could expect anything. This was a new culture to me and at my young age, I had to make some choices about where I stood. I did not know God was working on me then.

All of 1964 was training and we had many who went TTY to Indonesia, Cambodia and Vietnam. Rumors of the war were spreading and we could see the buildup coming. The training was getting more intense and I was growing up. I was becoming a man and as I grew, I had determined that I was going to make the best of it. I really was involved and trained hard, at the same time, I followed was around the wrong crowd and took up the habit of drinking or should I say, it took me over. By the end of 1964, I had spent two Christmas away from home and 1965 began with a bang. The rumors of what was taking place back in America were all over the base. More specially trained groups were going to Vietnam and causalities begun to take place. The training intensified and the motor pool was very busy getting vehicles and APC ready for war. Maintenance was a priority: Old engines in APC tracks were replaced, and other vehicles were be equipped for war.
In February of 1965, I had to return to states for a death in the family. It was only for about 10 days and the first thing I saw was men with long hair and a change in the moral structure. I could not believe the change and all that I had heard was taking place in the country.

In March of 1965, the war was heating up. The U.S. began bombing North Vietnam in March in "Operation Rolling Thunder." The U.S. Army and Marines began ground operations to ferret out and defeat the communist forces. General William Westmoreland commanded U.S. forces in South Vietnam. Westmoreland's strategy was attrition, employing U.S. superiority in firepower, technology, and mobility. The usual military tactics of the United States ground troops involved search and destroy operations. The larger units of U.S. military, South Vietnamese army supported by air and artillery, swept through an area to attempt to engage the communists in battle. North Vietnam and the Viet Cong, by contrast, relied on hit-and-run operations and ambushes, avoiding set-piece battles except at their own initiative. Political instability and internal dissent continued to plague the government of South Vietnam although in June General Nguyen Van Thieu and Air Marshall Nguyen Cao Ky took control of the country and remained in power for the remainder of the year. In the United States, a majority of Congress and the people supported U.S. participation in the war although protests against the war increased, especially among college students. The Clintons and many of those in Washington today were participants of those demonstrations.

[1]6–9 July: For us to understand the war we need to look at the following events that took place in 1965.

After B-52 strikes, the U.S. 173rd Airborne began another sweep through Zone D with 2,500 men and ARVN and Australian participation. The allies claimed to have inflicted 100 Viet Cong casualties.

8 July

Ambassador Maxwell Taylor resigned as U.S. Ambassador to South Vietnam. Taylor had earlier been opposed to the introduction of U.S. ground troops into South Vietnam, proposing instead an intensified air campaign against North Vietnam. Taylor would be replaced by Henry Cabot Lodge, Jr. who returned to Saigon for his second stint as Ambassador.

[2]10 July

---

[1] http://en.wikipedia.org/wiki/1965

[2] Adams, Sam (1994), War of Numbers: An Intelligence Memoir South Royalton, VT.: Steerforth Press.

Australia, Australian Defence Force (2010). "Australia in Vietnam" (PDF). Australian Defence Force. Retrieved March 29, 2010.

Bowman, John S., ed. (1985), The World Almanac of the Vietnam War, New York: Bison Books. ISBN 0-88687-272-3.

Buzzanco, Robert (1996), Masters of War: Military Dissent and Politics in the Vietnam Era, Cambridge, Cambridge University Press. ISBN 0-521-48046-9.

Clarke, Jeffrey J. (1988), The United States Army in Vietnam: Advice and Support: The Final Years, 1965-1973, Washington, D.C.: Center of Military History, United States Army.

Clodfelter, Michael (1995), Vietnam in Military Statistics: A History of the Indochina Wars, 1772-1991. McFarland & Company, 1995. ISBN 0786400277, 9780786400270

Fall, Bernard (1966), "Viet Nam in the Balance", The Australian Quarterly, Vol 38, No. 4, p. 13

FRUS. Foreign Relations of the United States, 1964-1968, Vol II, Vietnam, January–June 1965, United States Department of State, http://history.state.gov/historicaldocuments/frus1964-68v02

FRUS Foreign Relations of the United States, 1964-1968, Vol III, Vietnam, June–December 1965, United States Department of State, http://history.state.gov/historicaldocuments/frus1964-68v03

Garland, John M. (2000), Combat Operations: Stemming the Tide, May 1965 to October 1966, Washington, D.C.: Center of Military History, United States Army.

Heinemann, Larry (2006). Black Virgin Mountain: A Return to Vietnam (2006 ed.). Vintage Books. ISBN 1-4000-7689-7. - Total pages: 243

Jessup, John E. (1998). An encyclopedic dictionary of conflict and conflict resolution, 1945-1996 (1998 ed.). Greenwood Publishing Group. ISBN 0-313-28112-2. - Total pages: 887

Kaiser, David (2000), American Tragedy: Kennedy, Johnson, and the Origins of the Vietnam War, Cambridge: Harvard University Press. ISBN 0-674-00225-3.

Krepinevich, Jr., Andrew F. (1986), The Army and Vietnam, Baltimore: Johns Hopkins University Press. ISBN 0-8018-2863-5.

Li, Xiaobing (2007). A history of the modern Chinese Army (2007 ed.). University Press of Kentucky. ISBN 0-8131-2438-7. - Total pages: 413

Logevall, Frederik (1999), Choosing War: The Lost Chance for Peace and the Escalation of War in Vietnam Berkeley: University of California Press. ISBN 978-0-52022-919-8.

Lunch, William L. and Sperlich, Peter W. (1979), "American Public Opinion and the War in Vietnam" The Western Political Quarterly, Vol 32, No. 1, pp. 231–44. Downloaded from JSTOR.

The New York Times reported that the 173rd Airborne suffered 10 killed and 42 wounded on its sweep through Zone D and that its estimates of Viet Cong casualties were inflated. The U.S., the newspaper said, had begun "to accept aerial estimates of enemy casualties. The command has also begun to calculate probable damage inflicted on the Viet Cong despite the absence of bodies or weapons."

12 July

The 2nd Brigade of the U.S. 1st Infantry Division began to arrive in South Vietnam. The brigade was initially

McMaster, H. R. (1997), Dereliction of Duty: Lyndon Johnson, Robert McNamara, the Joint Chiefs of Staff and the Lies that Led to Vietnam, New York: Harper Perennial. ISBN 0-06-018795-6.

Mann, Robert (2001), A Grand Delusion: America's Descent into Vietnam, New York: Basic Books. ISBN 0-465-04369-0.

The Military History Institute of Vietnam (2002) Victory in Vietnam: The Official History of the People's Army of Vietnam, 1954-1975 Lawrence: University Press of Kansas. ISBN 0-7006-1175-4.

Moyar, Mark (2006), Triumph Forsaken: The Vietnam War, 1954–1965. New York: Cambridge University Press. ISBN 978-0-521-86911-9.

Qiang Zhai (1999), "Opposing Negotiations: China and the Vietnam Peace Talks, 1965-1968", Pacific Historical Review, Vol 68, No. 1. Downloaded from JSTOR.

Shulimson, Jack and Johnson, Major Charles M. (1978), U.S. Marines in Vietnam: The Landing and Building, 1965, Washington: Government Printing Office.

Summers, Jr., Harry G. (1985), Vietnam War Almanac, New York: Facts on File Publications. ISBN 0-8160-1017-X.

Tucker, Spencer C., ed. (2000), Encyclopedia of the Vietnam War: A Political, Social and Military History, Santa Barbara, California: ABC-CLIO. ISBN 978-1-57607-040-6.

United States, Government (2010). "Statistical information about casualties of the Vietnam War". National Archives and Records Administration. Archived from the original on 26 January 2010. Retrieved March 6, 2010.

Van Staaveren, Jacob (2002), Gradual Failure: The Air War Over North Vietnam 1965-1966, Washington: Air Force History and Museums Program, United States Air Force.

responsible for providing security for Bien Hoa air base near Saigon.

16 July
Secretary of Defense McNamara visiting South Vietnam and was briefed by MACV commander General Westmoreland. Westmoreland said that U.S. airstrikes had not succeeded in halting the flow of military supplies down the Ho Chi Minh trail. To defeat the Viet Cong, now reinforced by the North Vietnamese Army, would require another large influx of U.S. soldiers amounting to 57 battalions plus helicopter companies and support units. Westmoreland said he planned to reverse the deteriorating military situation by the end of 1965, take the offensive in 1966, and destroy the Viet Cong and capture their strongholds by the end of 1967.

20 July
McNamara returned to Washington and recommended to President Johnson that the number of U.S. troops in South Vietnam be increased to 175,000. He recommended also that 235,000 soldiers in the Reserve and National Guard be activated and that the number of U.S. military personnel be increased by 375,000. He recommended also that air strikes against North Vietnam be increased from 2,500 to 4,000 per month.

20 July
On the 11th anniversary of the signing of the Geneva Accords ending the First Indochina War, North Vietnamese leader Ho Chi Minh said that the North Vietnamese and the Viet Cong will fight for 20 years or more to achieve victory and unification of the two Vietnams.

21 July
Members of the New Zealand armed forces were deployed to South Vietnam.

24 July
The first surface-to-air missile (SAM) fired by North Vietnam brought down a U.S. F-4C Phantom jet. The SAM site that fired the missile was one of five ringing Hanoi at a distance of about 20 miles (32 km).

27 July
In a meeting with President Johnson, most Congressional leaders of both parties agreed with his plan to increase U.S. military forces in South Vietnam. The exception was Senator Mike Mansfield, while publicly supporting the President said at the meeting, said, "We are going deeper into a war in which even a total victory would, in the end, be a loss to the nation." Mansfield proposed negotiations to end the war.

28 July
President Johnson ordered an increase in the number of U.S. troops in South Vietnam to 125,000 and an increase in the draft of young Americans into the military from 17,000 to 35,000 per month, but he declined to activate the Reserve and National Guard. Johnson's announcement represented a quantum leap in the American commitment and was followed quickly by massive increases in the number of U.S. troops deployed to South Vietnam.

29 July
A brigade of the 101st Airborne Division arrived at Cam Rahn Bay and set up its base camp there.

August 1

The first U.S. Marines to arrive in South Vietnam in 1965 were based in I Corps at Danang. Their biggest battle in 1965, Operation Starlite, took place a few miles south of the city of Chu Lai.
Sixty-one percent of Americans responded "no" to the following question by the Gallup Poll, "Do you think the U.S. made a mistake sending troops to fight in Vietnam?"

U.S. Marines from H Company, 2nd Battalion, 7th Marines on patrol near Danang in 1965.

3 August
A company-sized U.S. Marine sweep through the village of Cam Ne was publicized in the U.S. A Marine was shown on television lighting an old woman's house while she pleaded for him to stop. The Marines said that the village had been fortified by the Viet Cong.

5 August
The Viet Cong attacked a petroleum storage facility near Danang, destroying 40 percent of the facility and almost 2 million gallons of fuel.

5 August
Former General and Ambassador Maxwell Taylor, now an adviser to President Johnson, told the President: "By the end of 1965, the North Vietnamese offensive will be bloodied and defeated without having achieved major gains." North Vietnam would be forced to change its strategy.

10–17 August
The U.S. Special Forces Civilian Irregular Defense Group (CIDG) camp at Duc Co, 45 kilometres (28 mi) southwest of Pleiku had been under siege by the Viet Cong since June. Attempts by ARVN to lift the siege had failed. General Westmoreland sent the 173rd airborne brigade to Pleiku and the brigade opened the highway from Pleiku to Duc Co. The Viet Cong, possibly reinforced by a North Vietnamese Unit, withdrew.

17–24 August
Operation Starlite was the first offensive military action conducted by the U.S. Marines during the Vietnam War and the first purely American operation. Lieutenant General Lewis W. Walt with 5,500 Marines launched a

preemptive strike against 1,500 Viet Cong to nullify a threat on the Chu Lai base, 60 miles (97 km) south of Danang. The Marines claimed to have killed more than 600 Viet Cong at a loss to themselves of more than 50 dead.

General William E. DePuy at a later briefing said that the Viet Cong "maneuvered in the jungle, maintained tactical integrity, withdrew their wounded, lost practically no weapons, and did a first class job" and that "we'd be proud of American troops...who did as well."

In August of 1965, we received orders we were going to Vietnam. The base was shut down and no one could leave. We started preparing and November we were on ships going to Vietnam. I spent my third Christmas away from home but this time it was in a staging area just outside of Saigon. I was now engaged in the war. This book is not about war but about liberty. America was now in full demonstration mode.
The events taking place in the states reflected on those who were drafted and coming to Vietnam. Many asked the question, "Why are we here?"

The following are some events that took place in 1965-1966.

11 September
The U.S. 1st Cavalry Division (Airmobile) began to arrive in South Vietnam at Qui Nhon. The division was the first full U.S. Army division to be deployed to South Vietnam. 1st Cavalry relied on helicopters to transport its combat units to and from operational areas.

13 September
Columnist Joseph Alsop said in the Washington Post said that, with the U.S. military build-up in South Vietnam, "at last there is light at the end of the tunnel."

18 September
In Operation Gibraltar 224 soldiers of the First Brigade of the 101st Airborne landed by helicopter near An Khe in the Central Highlands in an area in which two Viet Cong battalions were located. The Viet Cong attacked and killed 13 Americans. Air strikes forced the Viet Cong to retreat with losses estimated by the U.S. at between 226 to 257. General Westmoreland called the operation "a great victory." Others, including Col. David H. Hackworth, considered the battle "not...a great victory."

20 September
Seven U.S. warplanes were shot down over North and South Vietnam.

22 September
General Westmoreland requested 35,000 additional American troops which would bring the total military personnel authorized in South Vietnam to 210,000. President Johnson and Secretary of Defense McNamara set a limit of the total number of U.S. soldiers of 195,000.

The Plei Me Special Forces camp in 1965.

15 October
David Miller became the first American to burn his draft card as a protest against the Vietnam War. He was arrested by the FBI and later served 22 months in prison.

16 October
Protests against the U.S. participation in the Vietnam War took place in Europe and in about 40 U.S. cities. The organization coordinating the U.S. demonstrations was called the National Coordinating Committee to End the War in Vietnam.

19–25 October
The Siege of Plei Me was a series of assaults by the North Vietnamese army on a CIDG camp manned by U.S. and ARVN Special Forces and rangers and 400 Montagnard allies. U.S. airstrikes and a relief force lifted the siege. The siege led up to the Battle of Ia Drang.

27 October
A CIA intelligence estimate said, "Hanoi continues to asset its determination to press on with the war in South Vietnam despite the continuing attrition of the air war and the increase of US troops in the South."

2 November
To protest the Vietnam War a Quaker named Norman Morrison doused himself in kerosene and set himself on fire in front of The Pentagon. Morrison died.

3 November
In a memorandum to President Johnson, Secretary McNamara estimated total communist forces in South Vietnam as having increased to 230,000, including 71,000 Viet Cong main force, 40,000 political cadre, 110,000 guerrillas, and 20,000 North Vietnamese soldiers. McNamara anticipated that these totals would increase.

5–8 November
Operation Hump was a search and destroy operation by the 173rd Airborne Brigade, in an area about 17.5 miles north of Bien Hoa. The 1st Battalion, Royal Australian Regiment, deployed south of the Dong Nai River while the 1st Battalion, 503rd Infantry, conducted a helicopter assault on an LZ northwest of the Dong Nai and Song Be Rivers.

8 November
The Battle of Gang Toi was fought between Australian troops and the Viet Cong. The battle was one of the first engagements between the two forces during the war and occurred when the 1st Battalion, Royal Australian

Regiment (1RAR) found a Viet Cong bunker system in the Gang Toi Hills, in northern Bien Hoa Province.

8 November
A Republic of Korea army division completed its landing in South Vietnam to participate in the Vietnam War.[95] The Korean Division was stationed at Qui Nhon in Binh Dinh province on the central coast of South Vietnam. With the Koreans in Qui Nhon a brigade of the U.S. 1st Infantry Division moved inland to protect Highway 19 which led to Pleiku in the Central Highlands. A South Korean Marine Brigade was stationed at the port city of Neha Trang.

14–18 November
The Battle of Ia Drang was one of the most consequential battles of the Vietnam War. For the first time, the United States Army and the People's Army of Vietnam (the North Vietnamese Army) met head-on in a major engagement with the South Vietnamese army and the Viet Cong playing only minor roles. Casualties were heavy on both sides with some 250 U.S. and at least 1,200 North Vietnamese dead. For General Westmoreland the battle was a victory for U.S. firepower and mobility in a war of attrition in which the U.S. attempted to kill more communist troops than could be replaced. However, in the words of Joe Galloway, a journalist awarded a Bronze Star for his participation in the battle; Ia Drang was "the battle that convinced Ho Chi Minh he could win." The communists would "grind down the Americans" as they had the French in the 1940s and early fifties in the First Vietnam War.

30 November
In the aftermath of the Battle of Ia Drang and after meeting with General Westmoreland in South Vietnam, Secretary of Defense McNamara recommended in a memorandum to President Johnson that the number of U.S. troops in South Vietnam should be increased to about 400,000 in 1966

and possibly by an additional 200,000 in 1967. McNamara estimated that 1,000 Americans per month would die in the war and that "the odds are even" that the U.S. would prevail. McNamara recommended a pause in bombing North Vietnam of 3 to 4 weeks duration to try to find a way to end the war before undertaking the military buildup. Ambassador Lodge, General Westmoreland, and CINCPAC opposed the bombing halt.

18 December
Operation Game Warden (Task force 116) began. It was an U.S. and South Vietnamese Navy operation in the Mekong Delta and near Saigon to patrol the rivers and coastal waters of South Vietnam, prevent the infiltration of soldiers and supplies from North Vietnam, and deny the Viet Cong access to the waterways.

18 December
After a visit to South Vietnam, Marine Corps General Victor Krulak wrote a report expressing disagreement with General Westmoreland's strategy of attrition. It was "wasteful of American lives, promising a protracted, strength-sapping battle with small likelihood of a successful outcome." Krulak proposed instead a focus on a pacification program to provide village security plus increased air strikes.

24 December
President Johnson announced a halt in the bombing of North Vietnam and initiated a worldwide diplomatic effort to persuade North Vietnam to negotiate an end to the war. The Department of Defense opposed the bombing halt.

27 December
North Vietnamese leader Ho Chi Minh addressed the Communist Party Central Committee in Hanoi. Ho said that "politics" was the weak point of the American and South Vietnamese enemy and the domestic situation of the United States will not permit the U.S. to utilize its

military and economic power in South Vietnam. The Committee decided that the communist forces in South Vietnam should seek a "decisive victory within a relatively short period of time" but must prepare to defend itself if the U.S. expands its war effort.

31 December
The number of U.S. military personnel in South Vietnam totaled 184,314 compared to 23,310 at the end of 1964.U.S. casualties in 1965 totaled 1,928 dead compared to 216 in the previous year. South Vietnamese military forces totaled 514,000 including the Army and the Popular Force and Regional Force militias. The South Vietnamese armed forces suffered 11,242 killed in action, a five-fold increase in battle deaths since 1960. 93,000 persons deserted from South Vietnam's armed forces in 1965.

The North Vietnamese army at year's end numbered 400,000 compared to 195,000 at the end of 1964. Air force and air defense capabilities also were greatly expanded. 50,000 North Vietnamese cadre and soldiers infiltrated South Vietnam during 1965, equal to the total number infiltrated from 1959 through 1964. Group 559, charged with transporting supplies down the Ho Chi Minh Trail to supply communist troops in both South Vietnam and Laos, was expanded to 24,400 personnel and moved almost as much tonnage south in 1965 as it had in the preceding six years.

Conscription (draft) into the United States armed forces in 1965 was 230,991 men compared to 112,386 in 1964.

The events taking place in the states reflected on those who were drafted and coming to Vietnam. Many asked the question, "Why are we here?"

From September 1965 to January 1966, 170,000 men had been drafted and another 180,000 enlisted. By January, 2,000,000 men had secured college deferments.

February. Local artists in Hollywood build a 60-foot tower of protest on Sunset Boulevard.

March 25–26. It was the second day of International Protest organized by the National Coordinating Committee to End the War in Vietnam, led by SANE, Women Strike for Peace and the Committee for Nonviolent Action and the SDS: 20,000 to 25,000 in New York alone, demonstrations also in Boston, Philadelphia, Washington, Chicago, Detroit, and San Francisco, Oklahoma City. Demonstrations also took place abroad, in Ottawa, London, Oslo, Stockholm, Lyon, and Tokyo.

March 31. David Paul O'Brien and three companions burned their draft cards on the steps of the South Boston Courthouse. The case was later tried by the Supreme Court: "United States v. O'Brien."
In the spring clergy and laymen concerned about Vietnam was founded.

May 15. March Against the Vietnam War, led by SANE and Women Strike for Peace, with 8-10,000 taking part.
Muhammad Ali (Cassius Clay) refused to go to war, famously stating that he had "no quarrel with the Viet Cong" and that "no Viet Cong ever called me nigger." Ali also stated he would not go "10,000 miles to help murder, kill, and burn other people to simply help continue the domination of white slave masters over dark people." In 1967, he was sentenced to 5 years in prison, but was released on appeal by the United States Supreme Court.

The downfall of American liberty was taking place. When a nation of people cannot support the troops and people refuse to fight for their country you are on your way down. These demonstrations continued to the end of the war. By the end of 1966, I settled in to being at home. The war was raging and the streets of America were filled with demonstrators calling GI's baby killers. Those who were making it home wounded in heart and spirit hid in the crowd. One John Kerry went to Washington, spoke against the war, and betrayed his fellow soldiers. He had awarded himself two 'Silver Stars" Today he is "Secretary of State" Kerry was one of the key people who set up the agreement between the US, South Vietnam and North Vietnam. His agreement killed millions in Vietnam and set up one of the world's worst dictators in Cambodia. Poi Pot from 1963 to 1981, he served as the General Secretary of the Communist Party of Kampuchea. As such, he became the leader of Cambodia on 17 April 1975, when his forces captured Phnom Penh. From 1976 to 1979, he also served as the prime minister of Democratic Kampuchea.

He presided over a totalitarian dictatorship that imposed a radical form of agrarian socialism on the country. His government forced urban dwellers to move to the countryside to work in collective farms and forced labour projects. The combined effects of executions, forced labour, malnutrition and poor medical care caused the deaths of approximately 25 percent of the Cambodian population. In all, an estimated 1 to 3 million people (out of a population of slightly over 8 million) died due to the policies of his four-year premiership.

The results of the Vietnam Era would change America and set up a new theory called surrender.   Because of the policies instilled by our governmental leaders and people, we as a nation have caused the unnecessary deaths of millions. Obama the president of the USA is about to do the same thing and God only knows the outcome.

Here we are 2015.. and after over 5000 deaths of our soldiers in Iraq the and country is in worst chaos then when we went into it to liberate it. We have lost our creditability around the world because one man refuses to stand for what our country has always stood for: LOYALITY…" God and Country"

Psalm 37:6 (KJV)
[6] And he shall bring forth thy righteousness as the light, and thy judgment as the noonday.

God is going to judge the leaders of the world for their actions. We need to pray for America.

Chapter 1

What it used to be

Many years ago, I attended Liberty University; the name of the school was Liberty Baptist College in those years. Dr Jerry Falwell was the pastor of the church and chancellor of the college. He had started "Moral Majority" in the seventies and he was very productive with his message of liberty. In 1982, I got involved and became the state chairperson for the state of Indiana. If there was ever a man who loved his country it was Dr Falwell. While attending the college I had the privilege of taking part in the "I love America" rallies around the country. Watching Falwell motivated me to get more involved in the political side of things; Serving in Vietnam 1965-66 caused me to be a little gun shy when it came to people and politics. The nation was heading in the wrong direction and needed a president to take it in another direction. President Jimmy Carter had taken the nation into financial default with interest rates as high as 19% in some parts of the country. He had come into office in 1977 and was running for his second term in 1981. Ronald Reagan was running against him and Dr Falwell got behind Reagan and pushed the Christians to look at him and then vote for him.

Falwell made the following statement: [3] Mixing religion and politics can mean many things. It could mean that one advocates a theocratic state. I certainly do not. Such a merger of religion and politics is as far removed from my position as it is opposite, namely, a political system like communism, which represses religious thought and expression.

---

[3] Jerry Falwell in "The Baptists: A People Who Gathered 'To Walk in All His Ways,' " *Christian History*, no. 6.
Today's Best Illustrations - Today's Best Illustrations – Volumes 1-4.

Strangling of American Liberty

I firmly believe it is a religious duty to be a good citizen. It is one's duty as a good citizen to participate in politics, but I can be true neither to my country nor to my God if I separate my religious convictions from my political views. If I am to be whole, one with myself and with God, I must infuse my life as a political being with beliefs I learned from the Divine Being. This is not radical, fundamentalist Christian theory. It is the basic belief, which first drove the Pilgrims to our shores and later inspired the Founding Fathers to proclaim our independence from Britain "with a firm reliance on the protection of Divine Providence." It is the notion which infused the antislavery movement of the 19th century, and in which the Reverend Martin Luther King, Jr. took his message of racial harmony.

Why should we not permit moral values to influence our thinking about important contemporary issues? To say that spiritual values or morality is at the heart of our society is not to establish a state religion. Far from it: It is only to say with the Constitution that we guarantee the fundamental right of free exercise for all religions throughout our society...

My position-and I believe it is the position of the majority of Americans today, just as it has been for 200 years-is that it is not only legitimate to advocate basic religious values in the political arena, but it is absolutely essential for the health of our republic that believers participate in the political debate of our days.

It is our right and privilege to get involved in our country and politics are just part of this involvement. As a pastor, teacher, evangelist and

*citizen I have that right and I encourage you to
get involved."*

It is now 2015 and we have watched our nation move totally left of our values and principals.

The following are a few statements made by leaders and people of influence in the founding of this country.

- ***We hold these truths to be self-evident: that all men are created equal; that they are endowed by their Creator with certain unalienable rights; that among these are life, liberty, and the pursuit of happiness.***
  Thomas Jefferson

- ***They who can give up essential liberty to obtain a little temporary safety deserve neither liberty nor safety.***
  Benjamin Franklin

- ***Rightful liberty is unobstructed action according to our will within limits drawn around us by the equal rights of others. I do not add 'within the limits of the law' because law is often but the tyrant's will, and always so when it violates the rights of the individual.***
  Thomas Jefferson

- ***Democracy and socialism have nothing in common but one word, equality. But notice the difference: while democracy seeks equality in liberty, socialism seeks equality in restraint and servitude.***
  Alexis de Tocqueville

Our liberty is at stake more than any other time in our history. Due to a liberal Congress and liberal President in the last six years, our country no longer considered by other countries as the lighthouse on the hill.

The right of nature... is the liberty each man hath to use his own power, as he will himself, for the preservation of his own nature; that is to say, of his own life.
Thomas Hobbes

Government is supposed to be controlled by the people not politicians. The politician represents the people in his or her district or state. They should give the views of those he or she represents. Politicians make promises to get in office and then make deals with other political leaders to promote their agenda. The people are the last to hear about the deal and when these deals are made, it is too late for people to step in. It is all about power, the politicians know that. This is why they stay in office for years and get fat on the taxpayers money. Now, let me say, "Not all of these political leaders are corrupted but, through time and deal making they become corrupted." The democrats continue to push their liberal agenda and the American people can only follow their decision.

Our "Greatest Generation" fought and served our country in WWII. Back then, Movie Stars and Hollywood leaped at the chance to serve or entertain our troops overseas. Today they falsely exaggerate what an unsuccessful "quagmire" we are in, as they have done since North Korea, Vietnam and first Gulf War. Reliving 60's glory days, todays liberals are so bent on their own political power that they gush with every piece of bad news that comes out of Iraq, as anything that is bad, is great for them. Blinded by their hatred for conservative / Christian America, liberals twist and pervert even the most hideous attack on America as something that our President has done to us. A claim that is astronomically deceitful and underhanded. "No blood for oil" becomes a rally cry for those wanting political revenge for a close election (err, "stolen") and a Presidential sex scandal. The cost of weakening America and emboldening a hell-bent enemy sworn on our destruction is incidental to them. They do not care what other countries think about us. The on-sided Liberal Congress and Senate pushed Obama Care through with not one Republican vote.

The Black Caucus and Islamic leadership that are in Washington today have one desire to control America or destroy America.

The real question is who leads this country better, the Democrats or Republicans?

Under the Republicans Christian, values seem to be a big part of the platform, defense of country, less taxes, more responsibility given to the people and the rest of the world has respect for America. The Democrats base there platform on more government programs, taxes, less freedom, poorer relations with other countries, and the defense of the country takes second chair. Do you remember in 2006 at the Democratic National Convention they voted God out of the platform? Because of all of this, our liberty is being strangled.

Can you imagine what our founding fathers would have to say about today's politics? We have very few statesmen yet we have many salesmen and lawyers. Special interest groups, criminals who have gained control because they have money, control Washington. Unions control corruption in Washington. These abusers of the law buy people, power and security for their wrong doings. The American people are blinded by the back room deals, and abuse of taxpayer's money.

> *Liberty may be endangered by the abuse of liberty, but also by the abuse of power.*
> *James Madison*

Strangling of American Liberty

The government is so out of control. It is so bloated and infested with fraud, deceit, corruption, and abuse of power. Ted Nugent

The Obama administration came into Utah and said, 'We're not going to listen to what the U.S. Supreme Court said. 'We, the federal government, are going to recognize marriages in the state of Utah and Utah state law explicitly does not recognize as marriage,' and that was really, in my view, an abuse of power.
Ted Cruz

We are now at critical stage with abuse of power.

We have been warned yet we heed not to the warnings.[4]

Liberty may be endangered by the abuse of liberty, but also by the abuse of power.
- James Madison

Power without abuse loses its charm.
- Paul Valery

Anyone entrusted with power will abuse it if not also animated with the love of truth and virtue, no matter whether he be a prince, or one of the people.
- Jean de La Fontaine

But constant experience shows us that every man invested with power is apt to abuse it, and to carry his authority as far as it will go.
- Charles de Secondat

The right of self-defense never ceases. It is among the most sacred, and alike necessary to nations and to individuals, and whether the attack be made by Spain herself or by those who abuse her power,

---

[4] http://www.quotes-encouraging.com/quotes/abuse_power

its obligation is not the less strong.
- James Monroe

Every American, regardless of their background,
has the right to live free of unwarranted government
intrusion.
Repealing the worst provisions of the Patriot Act will
reign in this gross abuse of power and restore to everyone
our basic Constitutional rights.
- Pete Stark

Ukraine had quite serious impact on the many Russians.
They could see that ordinary people in Ukraine which is a
bordering state,
very close to Russia, the people of this state are,
they didn't want to tolerate anymore the power abuse by
Ukrainian officials.
- Garry Kasparov

Simply do your best, and you will avoid
self-judgment, self-abuse and regret.
- don Miguel Ruiz

We should meet abuse by forbearance.
Human nature is so constituted that
if we take absolutely no notice of anger or abuse,
the person indulging in it will soon weary of it and stop.
- Mohandas (Mahatma) Gandhi

Any informed borrower is simply less vulnerable to fraud
and abuse.
- Alan Greenspan

We expect teachers to handle teenage pregnancy,
substance abuse, and the failings of the family.
Then we expect them to educate our children.
- John Sculley

The real sin against life is to abuse and destroy beauty,
even one's own even more, one's own,
for that has been put in our care and we are responsible
for its well-being.
- Katherine Anne Porter

Strangling of American Liberty

Lawsuit abuse is a major contributor to the increased costs of healthcare,
goods and services to consumers.
- Charles W. Pickering

Democracy is an abuse of statistics.
- Jorge Luis Borges

If you want that good feeling that comes from doing things for other folks then you have to pay for it in abuse and misunderstanding.
- Zora Neale Hurston

Let us not forget who we are.
Drug abuse is a repudiation of everything America is.
- Ronald Reagan

What white man has ever seen me drunk? Who has ever come to me hungry and left me unfed? Who has seen me beat my wives or abuse my children? What law have I broken?
- Sitting Bull

Pity those who nature abuses; never those who abuse nature.
- Richard Brinsley Sheridan

We have copped a lot of ignorant abuse in the past, but it makes you wonder when a former state coroner openly attacks Aboriginal families who have been through hell.
- Arthur Murray

This China trade deal is basically like the Bobby Knight of trade deals.
You know, you abuse, you abuse, you abuse, and then they say 'Well, OK, we'll let you try one more time.'
- David Bonior

Looking back in history is a frightful look when you see were we have come from, liberty to abusive power. **David Smeltz**

As a preacher, I can remember when you could go on any street corner and preach the Gospel of Christ. Try that today and you will go to jail, while in the Philippines and even in Western Ukraine you can do it.

Children cannot pray in schools and prayers cannot be quoted in most public forum. I am the Chaplain of the Vietnam Veterans of America, State of Virginia and I received a letter not to end my prayers in "Jesus Name."

[5]I found the following on the internet.

Should Students Pray in Public Schools?

Public schools exist to educate, not to proselytize. Children in public schools are a captive audience. Making prayer an official part of the school day is coercive and invasive. What 5, 8, or 10-year-old could view prayers recited as part of class routine as "voluntary"? Religion is private, and schools are public, so it is appropriate that the two should not mix. To introduce religion in our public schools builds walls between children who may not have been aware of religious differences before.

This will give you just a little opinion of the anti-god crowd.

We should have as much privilege to pray as those who do not want to pray. I thought freedom of expression was part of our constitutional right. Does this not fall under freedom of speech?

[5] http://ffrf.org/publications/brochures/item/14113-schoolprayer

Chapter 2

A Disgrace to Our Military

In June of 2014, the President was involved in the release of Bowe Bergdahl a traitor in the US Army. That same month he filed an executive order: Executive Order -- 2014 Amendments to the Manual for Courts-Martial, United States. The following is the executive order he filed.

2014 AMENDMENTS TO THE MANUAL FOR COURTS-MARTIAL, UNITED STATES

[6]By the authority vested in me as President by the Constitution and the laws of the United States of America, including chapter 47 of title 10, United States Code (Uniform Code of Military Justice, 10 U.S.C. 801-946), and in order to prescribe amendments to the Manual for Courts-Martial, United States, prescribed by Executive Order 12473 of April 13, 1984, as amended, it is hereby ordered as follows:

Section 1. Part II, the Discussion for Part II, and the Analysis for Part II of the Manual for Courts-Martial, United States, are amended as described in the Annex attached and made a part of this order.
Sec. 2. These amendments shall take effect as of the date of this order, subject to the following:
(a) Nothing in these amendments shall be construed to make punishable any act done or omitted prior to the effective date of this order that was not punishable when done or omitted.

---

[6]   http://www.whitehouse.gov/the-press-office/2014/06/13/executive-order-2014-amendments-manual-courts-martial-united-states

(b) Nothing in these amendments shall be construed to invalidate any non-judicial punishment proceedings, restraint, investigation, referral of charges, trial in which arraignment occurred, or other action begun prior to the effective date of this order, and any such non-judicial punishment, restraint, investigation, referral of charges, trial, or other action may proceed in the same manner and with the same effect as if these amendments had not been prescribed.

Why would the president sign this order? Was this in conjunction with his release and deal with the Taliban?

In July of 2014, President Obama expanded the rights of Gays opening the door to marriage of gays.

[7]**Executive Order -- Further Amendments to Executive Order 11478, Equal Employment Opportunity in the Federal Government, and Executive Order 11246, Equal Employment Opportunity**

EXECUTIVE ORDER

FURTHER AMENDMENTS TO EXECUTIVE ORDER 11478, EQUAL EMPLOYMENT OPPORTUNITY IN THE FEDERAL GOVERNMENT, AND EXECUTIVE ORDER 11246, EQUAL EMPLOYMENT OPPORTUNITY

By the authority vested in me as President by the Constitution and the laws of the United States of America, including 40 U.S.C. 121, and in order to provide for a uniform policy for the Federal Government to prohibit discrimination and take further steps to promote economy and efficiency in Federal Government procurement by

---

[7] http://www.whitehouse.gov/the-press-office/2014/07/21/executive-order-further-amendments-executive-order-11478-equal-employmen

prohibiting discrimination based on sexual orientation and gender identity, it is hereby ordered as follows:

Section 1. Amending Executive Order 11478. The first sentence of section 1 of Executive Order 11478 of August 8, 1969, as amended, is revised by substituting "sexual orientation, gender identity" for "sexual orientation".

Sec. 2. Amending Executive Order 11246. Executive Order 11246 of September 24, 1965, as amended, is hereby further amended as follows:

(a) The first sentence of numbered paragraph (1) of section 202 is revised by substituting "sex, sexual orientation, gender identity, or national origin" for "sex, or national origin".

(b) The second sentence of numbered paragraph (1) of section 202 is revised by substituting "sex, sexual orientation, gender identity, or national origin" for "sex or national origin".

(c) Numbered paragraph (2) of section 202 is revised by substituting "sex, sexual orientation, gender identity, or national origin" for "sex or national origin".

(d) Paragraph (d) of section 203 is revised by substituting "sex, sexual orientation, gender identity, or national origin" for "sex or national origin".

Sec. 3. Regulations. Within 90 days of the date of this order, the Secretary of Labor shall prepare regulations to implement the requirements of section 2 of this order.

Sec. 4. General Provisions. (a) Nothing in this order shall be construed to impair or otherwise affect:

(i) the authority granted by law to an agency or the head thereof; or

(ii) the functions of the Director of the Office of Management and Budget relating to budgetary, administrative, or legislative proposals.

(b) This order is not intended to, and does not, create any right or benefit, substantive or procedural, enforceable at law or in equity by any party against the United States, its departments, agencies, or entities, its officers, employees, or agents, or any other person.

Sec. 5. Effective Date. This order shall become effective immediately, and section 2 of this order shall apply to contracts entered into on or after the effective date of the rules promulgated by the Department of Labor under section 3 of this order.

The president has decided to downsize our military. He has fired or forced retirement on many of generals. He is forcing retirement on many veterans with fifteen or more years.

[8]The purpose of this purge tended to vary depending on what the source of the list was. For ultra-conservative websites like World Net Daily and Breitbart, it was because the officers had dared express dissent against a President who hates America, and in particularly, hates the men and women of the Armed Forces. **For conspiracy-driven sites like Before It's News and Info wars, it was because Obama was on the verge of declaring martial law and these officers would not participate in the killing of American citizens.**

We have seen in many other circumstances how conspiracy theorists love to make lists of people related to some kind of catastrophe. In addition, a President liquidating the leadership of his military to make way for a

---

[8] http://skeptoid.com/blog/2014/03/24/president-obama-purge-military/

fascist takeover would indeed be a catastrophe. Nevertheless, is that what happened with these officers?

Two lists have been going around: One of nine officers and the other of 200 supposedly fired by President Obama during his entire presidency. The downsizing is affecting the everyday operation of the military.

I visited an army base in Georgia and talked with several noncommissioned officers who personally told me they had received notice of orders of discharge. Others had received orders to go back to Afghanistan for one year and then discharged. Some have claimed Obama wants to build his own army. Whatever is taking place the president has lost the respect of many in the military. Carter and Clinton were the last presidents to cut our military. Under Clinton, many military bases were closed in the states.

If our nation was to go to war the draft would have to start up for our military is hurting for leadership. This is what happened after the Vietnam War. Our military took years to rebuild. Once again, all of this is strangling our liberty.

The following article is important I took off the Department of Defense website.

[9]WASHINGTON — Defense Secretary Chuck Hagel plans to shrink the United States Army to its smallest force since before the World War II buildup and eliminate an entire class of Air Force attack jets in a new spending proposal that officials describe as the first Pentagon budget to aggressively push the military off the war footing adopted after the terror attacks of 2001.

The proposal, released on Monday, takes into account the fiscal reality of government austerity and the political reality

---

[9] Department of Defense February 24, 2014

of a president who pledged to end two costly and exhausting land wars. A result, the officials argue, will be a military capable of defeating any adversary, but too small for protracted foreign occupations. Officials who saw an early draft of the announcement acknowledge that budget cuts will impose greater risk on the armed forces if they are again ordered to carry out two large-scale military actions at the same time: Success would take longer, they say, and there would be a larger number of casualties. Officials also say that a smaller military could invite adventurism by adversaries.

A spending plan that will be released Monday will be the first sweeping initiative set forth by Defense Secretary Chuck Hagel. Credit Susan Walsh/Associated Press

"You have to always keep your institution prepared, but you can't carry a large land-war Defense Department when there is no large land war," a senior Pentagon official said.

Outlines of some of the budget initiatives, which are subject to congressional approval, have surfaced, an indication that even in advance of its release the budget is certain to come under political attack. For example, some members of Congress, given advance notice of plans to retire air wings, have vowed legislative action to block the move, and the National Guard Association, an advocacy group for those part-time military personnel, is circulating talking points urging Congress to reject anticipated cuts. State governors are certain to weigh in, as well. In addition, defense-industry officials and members of Congress in those port communities can be expected to oppose any initiatives to slow Navy shipbuilding. Even so, officials said that despite budget reductions, the military would have the money to remain the most capable in the world and that Mr. Hagel's proposals have the endorsement of the Joint Chiefs of Staff. Money saved by reducing the number of personnel, they said, would assure that those remaining in uniform would be well trained and supplied with the best weaponry.

The new American way of war will be underscored in Mr. Hagel's budget, which protects money for Special Operations forces and cyber warfare. And in an indication of the priority given to overseas military presence that does not require a land force, the proposal will — at least for one year — maintain the current number of aircraft carriers at 11. Over all, Mr. Hagel's proposal, the officials said, is designed to allow the American military to fulfill President Obama's national security directives: to defend American territory and the nation's interests overseas and to deter aggression — and to win decisively if again ordered to war.

"We're still going to have a very significant-sized Army," the official said. "But it's going to be agile. It will be capable. It will be modern. It will be trained." Mr. Hagel's plan would most significantly reshape America's land forces — active-duty soldiers as well as those in the National Guard and Reserve. The Army, which took on the brunt of the fighting and the casualties in Afghanistan and Iraq, already was scheduled to drop to 490,000 troops from a post-9/11 peak of 570,000. Under Mr. Hagel's proposals, the Army would drop over the coming years to between 440,000 and 450,000. That would be the smallest United States Army since 1940. For years, and especially during the Cold War, the Pentagon argued that it needed a military large enough to fight two wars simultaneously — say, in Europe and Asia. In more recent budget and strategy documents, the military has been ordered to be prepared to decisively win one conflict while holding off an adversary's aspirations in a second until sufficient forces could be mobilized and redeployed to win there.

The Guard and Reserves, which proved capable in their wartime deployments although costly to train to meet the standards of their full-time counterparts, would face smaller reductions. Nevertheless, the Guard would see its arsenal reshaped. The Guard's Apache attack helicopters would be transferred to the active-duty Army, which would transfer its Black Hawk helicopters to the Guard. The rationale is that Guard units have less peacetime need for the bristling array of weapons on the Apache and would put the Black Hawk — a workhorse transport helicopter — to use in domestic disaster relief. The cuts proposed by Mr. Hagel fit the Bipartisan Budget Act reached by Mr. Obama and Congress in December to impose a military spending cap of about $496 billion for fiscal year 2015. If steeper spending reductions kick in again in 2016 under the sequestration law, however, then even more cuts that are significant would be required in later years. The budget is the first sweeping initiative that bears Mr. Hagel's full imprint. Although Mr. Hagel has been in office one year, most of his efforts in that time have focused on initiatives and problems that he inherited. In many ways, his budget provides an opportunity for him to begin anew. The proposals are certain to face resistance from interest groups like veterans' organizations, which oppose efforts to rein in personnel costs; arms manufacturers that want to reverse weapons cuts; and some members of Congress who will seek to block base closings in their districts. Mr. Hagel will take some first steps to deal with the controversial issue of pay and compensation, as the proposed budget would impose a one-year salary freeze for general and flag officers; basic pay for military personnel would rise by 1 percent. After the 2015 fiscal year, raises in pay will be similarly restrained, Pentagon officials say.

In the meantime, Hagel has resigned and was asked to resign by President Obama. Why, because I think Hagel realized the prognosis. Obama only keeps those who follow him and obey his every command. Obama refuses to hear "NO" from anyone. This is why he said, "He had a phone and a pen" He has used both many times.

Notice the part of transferring equipment from the regular army to the reserves. Obama has tried to build a brown shirt army from the beginning and this could be the means to control the people. With Obama firing all of the important generals, he will only have reservist. These part time soldiers were drawn into the war full time. These men and woman have fought for our country and many have died. They need to be honored for their service. What we need to do is take one of those jets away from the Obama clan, sell it, and give the money to those who serve in the guard.

Iran has a plan to destroy the US

[10]A top commander of Iran's Revolutionary Guards boasted that his forces have plans in place to attack the United States from within, should the U.S. attack the Islamic Republic.

"America, with its strategic ignorance, does not have a full understanding of the power of the Islamic Republic," Brig. Gen. Hossein Salami said in a **televised interview**. "We have recognized America's military strategy, and have arranged our abilities, and have identified centers in America [for attack] that will create a shock."

Reports indicate that terrorist Hezbollah forces — allies of Iran — have infiltrated the U.S. and have mapped out targets.

"We will conduct such a blow in which they [America] will be destroyed from within," Salami said.

This is the second warning by a high-ranking officer of the Guards in two weeks. The chief commander of the Guards, Maj. Gen. Mohammad Jafari, addressing Secretary of

---

[10]http://www.redflagnews.com/headlines/iranian-commander-we-have-infiltrated-the-us-and-have-mapped-out-targets

---

State John Kerry, **said on Jan. 24** that a direct conflict with America is the "strongest dream of the faithful and revolutionary men around the world."

Kerry had previously said that if Iran did not live up to the agreement reached in Geneva on its nuclear program, "all options are on the table."

"Your threats to revolutionary Islam are the best opportunity," Jafari had said. "Muslim leaders for years have been preparing us for a decisive battle…. Do you know how many thousands of revolutionary Muslims at the heart of the Islamic revolutionary groups around the world are awaiting for you to take this [military] option from the table into action?"

Gen. Salami went further, saying the Revolutionary Guards have taken into consideration America's military ability and different scenarios under which the U.S. could attack Iran via a limited missile or air strike, or even a ground attack.

"All operational bases of the enemy in the region in whatever capacity and location are within our firepower," Salami warned. "The American military option does not make a difference for us, and they can use this option, but they will have to accept the responsibility of devastating consequences."

Salami asked whether America could control the spread of any war with the Islamic Republic: "Can they preserve their vital interest in the region in the face of endless attacks by Iran? Can they keep their naval assets and the Zionist regime [Israel] secure?"

Salami said that with the U.S. economy and debt, America is in no position to engage Iran militarily.

The general then taunted Washington, citing Iran's political and cultural influence in Iraq. "The current has changed for

Strangling of American Liberty

the Americans so much so that they invest [by invading Iraq] and others [Iran] benefit."

For six years, President Obama has catered to Iran, what is going to take him to wake up. Every day the threat grows greater. **Proverbs 15:33 (KJV)** [33] The fear of the LORD *is* the instruction of wisdom; and before honour *is* humility. Where is the humility with President Obama?

Chapter 3

A Rebellious Generation

I am convinced the problems we are facing today began in the late fifties and sixties. The following is order of the presidents from 1953 to present. I think as you look at their accomplishment you will see the downfall of this nation.

- ❖ [11]34. Dwight D. Eisenhower (1953-1961)VP Richard Nixon (1953-1961)
- ❖ 35. John F. Kennedy (1961-1963) VP Lyndon B. Johnson (1961-1963)
- ❖ 36. Lyndon B. Johnson (1963-1969) None (1963-1965)
  VP Hubert Humphrey (1965-1969)
- ❖ 37. Richard Nixon (1969-1974)　VP Spiro Agnew (1969-1973)　Speaker of the House Gerald Ford (1973-1974)
- ❖ 38. Gerald Ford (1974-1977)　　NO VP (1974) Nelson Rockefeller (1974-1977)
- ❖ 39. Jimmy Carter (1977-1981) VP Walter Mondale (1977-1981)
- ❖ 40. Ronald Reagan (1981-1989)　VP George Bush (1981-1989)
- ❖ 41. George Bush (1989-1993) VP Dan Quayle (1989-1993)
- ❖ 42. Bill Clinton (1993-2001)　VP Al Gore (1993-2001)
- ❖ 43. George W. Bush (2001-2009)　VP Dick Cheney (2001-2009)
- ❖ 44. Barack Obama (2009-present) VPJoe Biden (2009-present)

You have it heard it said, "Everything rises and falls on leadership".

In my review, I believe we can go back to 1953; our governmental leaders have made decisions that have gone

---

[11] http://www.presidentsusa.net/presvplist.html

against the moral strain of this country. The wars in Vietnam and desegregation years brought about historical turmoil like no other time in our history. I would like to key on some main events that took place over this period with the Presidents, Congress and Senate in leadership. We have a two party system generally in this country. The democrats viewed as the liberal party and Republicans conservative in view. These two parties battle within and most of the time the people pay for the decisions they make. Elected by the people yet there representation is usually accomplished through bargaining. Every bill that is passed must pass through the Congress and Senate and go to the President's desk for approval or veto. The President has executive powers and can sign into power bills that never reach the Congress.

In the following statement, you will see many of the bills and legislation passed and vetoed by the President. Our liberty has been strangled because of such bills.

August 7, 1953 Eisenhower signs the Refugee Relief Act of 1953, admitting 214,000 more immigrants than permitted under existing immigration quotas.

August 19, 1953 Iranians, with the backing of the CIA, overthrow the government of Prime Minister Mohammed Mossadegh, ensuring Mohammed Reza Shah Pahlavi's hold on power.

October 8, 1953 Eisenhower announces that the Soviet Union has tested a hydrogen bomb.

President Kennedy did not serve a full four year term he was assassinated in his third year.

The following are some of the events and legislation he was involved in:

April 15-20, 1961, A U.S.-sponsored invasion of Cuba at the Bay of Pigs fails. With inadequate support and facing an overwhelming force, the CIA-trained brigade of anti-

Castro exiles is defeated in a few days. Kennedy takes responsibility for the disaster.

May 4, 1961 Black and white youths supported by the Congress of Racial Equality (CORE) set out on the "freedom rides" to test the enforcement of ICC rules against discrimination in interstate travel.

June 3, 1961 Kennedy meets with Soviet premier Nikita S. Khrushchev in Vienna. The conference fails to resolve conflict over the status of Berlin.

August 13, 1961 East Germany, supported by the Soviet Union, begins construction of the Berlin Wall, halting the flow of refugees to the West.

January 29, 1962 The Geneva conference, with the United States, Soviet Union, and the United Kingdom participating, adjourns without reaching an agreement on a nuclear test ban.

February 3, 1962 Kennedy halts virtually all trade with Cuba.

February 26, 1962 The U.S. Supreme Court rules that segregation in transportation facilities is unconstitutional.

February 30, 1962 Astronaut John Glenn becomes the first American to orbit the earth.

September 30, 1962 The U.S. Supreme Court orders the University of Mississippi to admit James H. Meredith, its first African-American student. After Governor Ross Barnett attempts to block the admission, U.S. Marshals escort Meredith to campus while Federalized national guardsmen maintain order.

October 16, 1962 Kennedy is informed of the existence of Soviet missile installations in Cuba.

Strangling of American Liberty

October 22, 1962 Kennedy addresses the American people about the situation in Cuba and orders a navel quarantine of Cuba to prevent further shipments of weapons.

October 28, 1962 After thirteen days, the Cuban Missile Crisis is resolved. The United States will pledge not to invade Cub (and secretly agrees to remove missiles from Turkey), in exchange for the removal of the Soviet weapons.

November 20, 1962 Kennedy lifts the naval blockade of Cuba.

April 3, 1963 Martin Luther King Jr leads a civil rights drive in Birmingham, Alabama. Police Commissioner Eugene "Bull" Connor orders the police to use fire hoses and dogs on demonstrators.

June 12, 1963 Medgar W. Evers, NAACP field secretary for Mississippi, is assassinated outside his home in Jackson.

June 26, 1963 Speaking in West Berlin, Kennedy demonstrates his solidarity with the city, declaring "Ich bin ein Berliner."

August 28, 1963 The March on Washington attracts 250,000 demonstrators to the nation's capital in support of civil rights legislation. At the Lincoln Memorial, Martin Luther King Jr. delivers his "I Have a Dream" speech.

September 15, 1963 Four young African-American girls are killed in the bombing of a church in Birmingham, Alabama.

October 7, 1963 Kennedy signs a limited nuclear test-ban treaty with the Soviet Union and the United Kingdom.

November 1, 1963 South Vietnamese President Ngo Dinh Diem is assassinated in U.S.-supported coup.

November 22, 1963 Kennedy is assassinated while riding in a motorcade in Dallas, Texas. Lee Harvey Oswald was arrested and accused of the crime. Vice President Lyndon Baines Johnson is sworn in as the thirty-sixth President of the United States following the assassination.

From 1961-1963 are known as the turmoil years.

The nation was dealing with turmoil in Europe and Asia and on top of all those problems; America had internal problems with de-segregation. The streets were full of fighting and families divided over so many issues. The nation needed leadership and President Johnson was not the man to take the helm. History has proved President Johnson made some major mistakes that led to the war in Vietnam.

Johnson takes over on November 23, 1963.

July 2, 1964, Johnson signs The Civil Rights Act of 1964.

August 4, 1964 three civil rights workers are found dead in Mississippi. James Chaney, Andrew Goodman, and Michael Schwerner were all participating in the Mississippi Freedom Summer.

❖ **August 7, 1964 Congress passes the Gulf of Tonkin Resolution giving the President power to pursue military action in Vietnam.**
October 14, 1964 Martin Luther King Jr. is awarded the Nobel Peace Prize.

October 15, 1964 Nikita Khrushchev is forced to resign as leader of the Soviet Union and is replaced by Leonid Brezhnev.

Strangling of American Liberty

November 3, 1964 Lyndon B. Johnson is elected President of the United States.

As we look into1965, we can see the turmoil grows and the demonstrations get bigger. Johnson is heading to war and by the end of 1965; the Pacific theatre is on its way to war.

January 20, 1965 Johnson is inaugurated President of the United States.

> ❖ *February 9, 1965 Nine American soldiers are killed in an attack on U.S. barracks in Pleiku, Vietnam. Johnson begins the bombing of North Vietnam.*

February 21, 1965 Malcolm X is assassinated by other black Muslims in New York City.

March 15, 1965 Johnson calls for voting rights legislation.

March 21, 1965 Martin Luther King Jr. leads a march from Selma to Montgomery, Alabama.

April 11, 1965 Johnson signs the Elementary and Secondary Education Act.

April 28, 1965 Johnson sends U.S. marines to the Dominican Republic to protect U.S. citizens after a military coup.

June 7, 1965 The U.S. Supreme Court finds a Connecticut law banning the use of contraceptives unconstitutional.

July 26, 1965 Martin Luther King Jr. leads a demonstration in Chicago in an attempt to bring the Civil Rights Movement to the North.

> ❖ *July 28, 1965 Johnson increases the number of troops sent to Vietnam, indicating his determination to engage in a ground war.*

July 30, 1965 Johnson signs legislation creating Medicare and Medicaid.

August, 1965 A paper by Daniel Patrick Moynihan, entitled, *The Negro Family: The Case For National Action*, is released. The conclusions of the "Moynihan Report" create heated controversy.

August 5, 1965 Johnson signs the Voting Rights Act into law.

August 11-16, 1965 The Watts Riots break out in Los Angeles.

From 1966 to 1968.. America has to make many transitions. As a nation the baby boomers are off to war, the streets in America are full of demonstration and the country is at war within its self.

February 21, 1966 Fearing that American involvement in Vietnam will draw France into a world war, French president Charles de Gaulle announces that France will withdraw from NATO.

March 7, 1966 The U.S. Supreme Court unanimously upholds the Voting Rights Act of 1965.

June 1-2, 1966 The White House Conference on Civil Rights urges Congress to pass further civil rights legislation.

June 6, 1966 James Meredith is shot in a March from Memphis, Tennessee, to Jackson, Mississippi; civil rights leaders organize to complete his march. During this demonstration, Stokely Carmichael makes a statement in support of "black power."

June 13, 1966 In *Miranda v. Arizona*, the U.S. Supreme Court rules that the constitutional provision against self-incrimination applies to police interrogations.

Strangling of American Liberty

October 1966 Huey P. Newton and Bobby Seale found the Black Panther Party in Oakland, California.

January 27, 1967 A launch pad fire during tests for the Apollo program kills three astronauts.

February 10, 1967 The Twenty-Fifth Amendment to the Constitution is ratified, providing rules of succession upon the death or incapacitation of the President, and enabling the President to appoint a new vice-president in the case of a vacancy.

> ❖ *June 5, 1967 The Six Day War breaks out between Israel and several Arab nations.*

June 14, 1967 Johnson appoints Thurgood Marshall to the Supreme Court.

> ❖ *July 13, 1967 Riots break out in Newark, New Jersey.*

> ❖ *July 23, 1967 Riots spread across the city of Detroit, Michigan.*

> ❖ *October 21, 1967 Anti-war demonstrators March to the Pentagon in an attempt to shut it down.*

January 22, 1968 North Korean forces capture the *U.S.S. Pueblo.*

> ❖ *January 30, 1968 North Vietnamese troops surprise South Vietnamese and American troops by attacking during the Tet holiday. While the Tet Offensive is not a military loss for the United States, it leads to a loss of confidence in the Johnson administration's prosecution of the war.*

March 12, 1968 Johnson wins the New Hampshire Democratic primary, but anti-war candidate Eugene McCarthy comes in a close second with 42 percent of the vote.

The disgrace of the nation takes place in the next five years as Nixon takes office. His example in the White House exceeds his authority. His Executive outreach in later years will be seen in another president who will use his tactics to control the country.

❖ *March 16, 1968 U.S. forces in Vietnam commit massacre in the hamlet of My Lai; hundreds of unarmed men, women, and children are killed. News of the event would not reach the public until November 1969.*

March 16, 1968 Robert Kennedy enters the race for the Democratic nomination for President.

March 31, 1968 Johnson announces a partial bombing halt and his unwillingness to seek re-election to the presidency.

April 4, 1968 Martin Luther King Jr. is assassinated in Memphis, Tennessee.

❖ **April 23, 1968** Students at Columbia University take over several buildings on campus.

April 29, 1968 Ralph Abernathy of the Southern Christian Leadership Conference (SCLC) begins the Poor People's Campaign in Washington, D.C.

May 13, 1968 The United States and North Vietnam begin peace talks in Paris.

June 5, 1968 Senator Robert Kennedy is assassinated *after winning the Democratic primary in California.*

❖ *In 1968, two very influential men were assassinated making it one of the worst years in history.*

Strangling of American Liberty

August 20-21, 1968 The Soviet Union invades Czechoslovakia to end the movement toward greater freedom and independence.

November 5, 1968 Richard M. Nixon is elected President of the United States, and Spiro Agnew is elected vice-president.

> *The events of 1964-1968 created the beginning of the rebellious nation. For the first time in the history of this great nation we are at war within and without our boundaries: Drugs are on the scene and people are confused about our future.*

November 12, 1968 Leonid Brezhnev announces that the Soviet Union has the right to intervene anywhere in its sphere of influence. This "Brezhnev Doctrine" becomes central to Soviet foreign policy.

January 20, 1969 Nixon is sworn into office as the thirty-seventh President of the United States.

❖ **March 4, 1969** Nixon warns that the United States will take action in the event of a new Viet Cong offensive.

April 18, 1969 Following an attack on a U.S. plane on April 15, Nixon orders that reconnaissance flights off North Korea be resumed.

April 30, 1969 Nixon asks that Congress be granted authority to consolidate federal aid programs to states and cities.

❖ **May 14, 1969** Nixon proposes a plan whereby the United States and North Vietnam would agree to withdraw forces from South Vietnam.

May 27, 1969 Nixon asks that Congress make the Post Office department a public corporation.

➢ **June 8, 1969** Nixon announces a plan to withdraw 25,000 U.S. troops from South Vietnam by August 31.

July 9, 1969 Nixon orders cuts in overseas government personnel by 10 percent.

➢ **July 25, 1969** Nixon affirms his desire to withdraw U.S. troops from southeast Asia and declares that individual nations will bear a larger responsibility for their own security. Initially referred to as the "Guam Doctrine," this statement later becomes known as the "Nixon Doctrine."

August 8, 1969 Nixon discloses his program for welfare reform, which includes the Family Assistance Plan.

October 31, 1969 Nixon declares that Latin America must be responsible for its own social and economic progress.

➢ **November 3, 1969** Nixon reveals that North Vietnam has rejected the administration's secret peace offers. He proposes a plan for the gradual and secretive withdrawal of troops.

November 26, 1969 Nixon signs the Selective Service Reform bill, ensuring that draftees are selected by a lottery system.

March 24, 1970 The administration announces that it will seek to end de jure segregation.

April 23, 1970 Nixon signs executive order ending occupational and parental deferments for the draft.

Strangling of American Liberty

July 9, 1970 Nixon puts forth a plan to reorganize the federal agencies that handle environmental problems.

July 20, 1970 Nixon states in a news conference that the United States would accept a coalition government in Vietnam if it were chosen in an open election.

July 23, 1970 Nixon approves a plan for an Interagency Committee on Intelligence to conduct operations against domestic targets.

September 18, 1970 Nixon meets with Israeli Premier Golda Meir to talk about problems in the Middle East.

October 7, 1970 In a televised address, Nixon proposes a five-point peace plan for Indochina. The plan includes a "cease-fire in place" and the negotiated withdrawal of U.S. troops from Vietnam.

December 31, 1970 Nixon signs a clean air bill, which mandates that car manufacturers reduce certain pollutants by 90 percent.

January 4, 1971 Nixon tells an ABC news commentator that he is now a "Keynesian."

January 19, 1971 Nixon delays the construction of the Cross-Florida Barge Canal in order to stop environmental damage.

February 16, 1971 Taping systems are activated in the White House. The Oval Office is outfitted with a voice-activated system and the Cabinet Room with a manual system.

April 6, 1971 A voice-activated taping system in the Executive Office Building (EOB) becomes operational. Taping also begins on phone conversations held in the Oval Office, the EOB, and the Lincoln Sitting Room.

➢ **June 13, 1971** The *New York Times* begins to publish secret internal documents referred to as the "Pentagon Papers," a development that leads the White House become increasingly fearful of further disclosures. Within a week, a special unit named the "Plumbers" is created to stop the leaks.

July 15, 1971 Nixon shocks the nation with the news that he plans to visit China within the next year.

August 15, 1971 Nixon declares a 90-day freeze on wages and prices, known as Phase 1 of his economic program.

October 7, 1971 Nixon announces Phase 2 of his economic plan.

December 9, 1971 Nixon vetoes legislation calling for the establishment of a national day-care system.

December 22, 1971 Nixon signs an extension of the Economic Stabilization Act, allowing himself another year in which to right the economy.

February 21-27, 1972 President and Mrs. Nixon arrive in China. A joint communique, later known as the Shanghai Communique, is released by the United States and China. It calls for both countries agree to increase their contacts, and for the United States to withdraw gradually from Taiwan.

February 28, 1972 Nixon addresses the nation via television to discuss his trip to China.

➢ **March 16, 1972** Nixon dismisses bussing as a means of achieving racial integration and seeks legislation that would deny court-ordered bussing.

➢ **May 8, 1972** On national television, Nixon states that he has ordered the mining of North Vietnamese ports and the bombing of military targets in the North Vietnam.

Strangling of American Liberty

May 16, 1972 The taping system attached to the telephone on the Camp David study table becomes operational.

May 17, 1972 A voice-activated taping system in Aspen Lodge at Camp David becomes operational.

May 18, 1972 The taping system attached to the telephone on the Camp David study desk becomes operational.

May 22, 1972 Nixon arrives in the Soviet Union for a summit meeting. He is the first sitting President to visit the U.S.S.R.

> ➤ **June 17, 1972** Police seize James McCord, Frank Sturgis, and three Cubans inside Democratic Headquarters in Washington, D.C.'s Watergate Hotel. They confiscate cameras, wiretapping materials, and $2,300 in cash.

June 23, 1972 Nixon orders Chief of Staff H.R. Haldeman to tell the F.B.I. not to go any further with its Watergate investigation, justifying his actions on national security grounds.

> ➤ **August 29, 1972** In a news conference, Nixon declares that no one on the White House staff, in the administration, or anyone "presently employed" was involved in the Watergate break-in.

October 30, 1972 Nixon signs sixty bills, one of which provides more than $5 billion in benefits for the aged, blind, and disabled, while also increasing Social Security taxes.

November 8, 1972

Nixon asks for the resignation of all agency directors, federal department heads, and presidential appointees.

January 27, 1973 Paris Peace Accords are signed by all parties at war in Vietnam.

March 4, 1973 The voice-activated taping system at Camp David ceases operation, as does the system attached to the desk telephone in the Camp David study.

> **April 30, 1973** Nixon admits responsibility for the Watergate affair on television, but continues to assert no prior knowledge of it.

June 21, 1973 The taping system attached to the table phone in the Camp David study ceases operation.

July 12, 1973 The voice-activated taping system in the Oval Office ceases operation.

July 16, 1973 Testifying before the Senate Watergate Committee, Federal Aviation administrator Alexander Butterfield confirms the existence of an Oval Office taping system.

July 18, 1973 Phase 4 of the economic program is revealed, in which the freeze is lifted on all foods except beef and health-care products.

July 18, 1973 The manual taping system in the Cabinet Room ceases operation, as do those attached to telephones in the Oval Office, the EOB, and the Lincoln Sitting Room.

> **July 23, 1973** claiming executive privilege, Nixon refuses to turn over subpoenaed tapes to the Senate Watergate Committee, chaired by Senator Sam Ervin (D-NC).

> **August 7-8, 1973** Vice President Agnew comes under scrutiny for charges stemming from campaign contributions he received while in office from persons who were later given government contracts. Agnew vehemently denies the charges in a press conference.

> **August 15, 1973** Nixon denies involvement in the Watergate cover-up in a televised address.

Strangling of American Liberty

October 10, 1973 Vice President Spiro Agnew resigns and pleads "no contest" to charges stemming from a kickback scheme he ran while Governor of Maryland. Agnew is fined $10,000 and sentenced to three years' probation.

October 12, 1973 Gerald Ford is nominated as vice president. After being confirmation by Congress, he is sworn in on December 6.

November 7, 1973 Nixon addresses the nation regarding the energy crisis.

December 21, 1973 Nixon increases Social Security benefits.

> **January 4, 1974** The Senate Watergate Committee subpoenas more than 500 tapes, which Nixon refuses to hand over, stating presidential communications must remain confidential.

January 30, 1974 Nixon gives his State of the Union address, in which he refuses to resign and demands an end to the Watergate investigation.

> **April 3, 1974** As a result of an IRS investigation into Nixon's finances, the President is forced to pay $432,787 in back taxes and $33,000 interest.

April 29, 1974 Nixon addresses the nation before disclosing more than 1,200 pages of his conversations regarding Watergate.

May 23, 1974 Despite Vice President Ford's advice to surrender the necessary evidence to the House Judiciary Committee, Nixon refuses to hand over Watergate-related tapes.

> **July 24, 1974** In an 8-0 ruling, the Supreme Court orders that Nixon turn over sixty-four tapes to the Senate Watergate Committee. The tapes disclose Nixon's knowledge and participation in the cover-up of the Watergate burglary.

- **July 27-30, 1974 Three articles of impeachment are brought against Nixon by the House Judiciary Committee: obstruction of justice, abuse of power, and the unconstitutional defiance of its subpoenas.**

August 5, 1974 Three new transcripts are released, showing that Nixon ordered a cover-up less than a week after the break-in. Nixon issues a statement with the transcripts indicating that he withheld this evidence from his lawyers and from those who support him on the Judiciary Committee.

August 6, 1974 Nixon informs his cabinet that he will not resign despite the fact that even his closest advisors are suggesting that he should.

August 7, 1974 Nixon is told by a few of his supporters that he would not win an impeachment trial. Nixon tells Kissinger, Ford, and a few Congressional leaders that he plans to resign.

- **August 8, 1974 Nixon resigns the presidency, effective at noon the next day, in a televised address.**

August 9, 1974 Nixon leaves for California. His letter of resignation is sent to Kissinger, thus making Gerald Ford the thirty-eighth President of the United States.

I left out the Ford years, as the unique part of his years in office was the pardon he gave to Nixon. The next president of interest is President Jimmy Carter.

The Peanut Farmer Takes over and just about destroys the nation.

Strangling of American Liberty

January 20, 1977 Carter is inaugurated the thirty-ninth President of the United States.

- ❖ **January 21, 1977** Carter pardons Vietnam War draft evaders. **(This was a kick in the face of the Vietnam Veterans and opened the door for those who did not want to serve to leave the country)**

February 2, 1977 Congress passes Emergency Natural Gas Act, authorizing the President to deregulate natural gas prices due to a shortage in supply. Carter signs the bill and announces plans to present an energy program to Congress. He later proposes the establishment of a cabinet-level Department of Energy.

February 15-21, 1977 Secretary of State Cyrus Vance travels to the Middle East in an attempt to reconvene the 1973 Geneva Conference.

April 18, 1977 In an address to the nation, Carter calls his program of energy conservation the "moral equivalent of war."

May 22, 1977 Carter speaks at Notre Dame University, presenting a new direction in foreign policy, which takes the focus off anti-Communism and emphasizes support for fundamental human rights.

June 20, 1977 Carter announces opposition to production of the B-1 strategic bomber.

July 19, 1977 Newly elected Israeli Prime Minister Menachem Begin meets with Carter in Washington.

December 29-31, 1977 Carter meets with Polish First Secretary Gierek in Warsaw.

December 31-January 1, 1977 Carter visits the Mohammed Reza Shah Pahlavi, in Tehran, calling Iran "an island of stability" in the Middle East.

January 1-6, 1978 Carter travels to India, Saudi Arabia, Egypt, France, and Belgium.

March 17, 1978 Carter warns of the Soviet threat in a foreign policy address at Wake Forest University.

June 7, 1978 Carter graduation speech at Annapolis emphasizes the importance of human rights in foreign policy.

September 5-17, 1978 Carter mediates talks between Prime Minister Menachem Begin of Israel and President Anwar Sadat of Egypt at Camp David, resulting in a peace treaty between the two nations.

December 15, 1978 The Carter administration grants full diplomatic status to the People's Republic of China.

April 20, 1979 President Carter claims a rabbit tried to attack him during a fishing trip in Georgia, and the *Washington Post* runs a front-page story with the headline: "President Attacked by Rabbit."

June 7, 1979 Carter approves development of the MX missile.

June 18, 1979 Carter signs the second Strategic Arms Limitation Treaty (SALT II) with the USSR. The U.S. Senate never ratifies the controversial treaty, although both nations voluntarily comply with its terms.

July 15, 1979 Carter delivers what becomes known as his "malaise speech," blaming the problems of the nation on "a crisis of spirit."

July 18-19, 1979 Carter accepts the resignations of five cabinet members and names Hamilton Jordan chief of staff.

September 14, 1979 A *Washington Post* poll gives Carter the lowest approval rating of any President in three decades.

November 4, 1979 Iranian students take sixty-six Americans hostage at the American embassy in Tehran.

January 3-4, 1980 Due to the invasion of

Afghanistan, Carter asks the Senate to table its consideration of SALT II. He also placed an embargo on grain sales to the Soviet Union and suggests the possibility of boycotting the Summer Olympics in Moscow.

January 23, 1980 Carter announces the "Carter Doctrine" in his State of the Union address, asserting that threats to the Persian Gulf region will be viewed as "an assault of the vital interests of the United States."

April 17, 1980 Carter announces that the economy is in recession, with the inflation rates hitting ten percent and interest rates climbing to eighteen percent.

April 25, 1980 Carter announces the failure of "Desert One," the mission to rescue the Iranian-held hostages, and that several American military personnel had been killed.

June 1980 Carter's approval rating reaches the lowest mark of any President since 1945.

November 4, 1980 Carter loses election to Ronald Reagan, winning only 49 electoral votes to Reagan's 489.

> *The Reagan years were the most productive years in our history as a nation.*

January 20, 1981

Ronald Reagan is inaugurated President, and Carter leaves Washington, D.C.

Reagan brings respect back to our nation. Under his leadership, we a tremendous financial recovery and the Cold war end. The wall between East and West Germany begins to come down and the Soviet Union is broken up and divided. He drew respect and other nations feared his leadership. He was elected with over 80% of the electoral votes.

January 20, 1989 George H. W. Bush is inaugurated as the forty-first President.

February 6, 1989 President Bush, at a White House press conference, introduces his bailout plan for troubled savings and loans banks. It provides for the sale of $50 billion in government bonds to finance the bailout and gives the Federal Deposit Insurance Corporation (FDIC) regulatory oversight over S&Ls.

> *This begins the new Era of war in the Arabic nations.*

March 14, 1989 The Bush administration, at the urging of federal drug czar, William Bennett, announces a temporary ban on the importation of semi-automatic rifles, a reversal of President Bush's earlier statements indicating that no restriction on these firearms would be enacted.

Strangling of American Liberty

➢ **March 24, 1989** *in the worst oil spill on American territory, the Exxon Valdez supertanker runs aground in southeastern Alaska. The tanker dumps 240,000 barrels of oil into the surrounding waters and causes extensive environmental damage.*

➢ **April 17, 1989** *President Bush offers a program of special assistance for Poland, whose Communist government has agreed to negotiations with the opposition Solidarity party, which produces plan free elections. Elections are held in August 1989, which lead to the end of single-party rule in Poland.*

June 4, 1989 The People's Liberation Army, the military arm of the Chinese government, uses tanks and armored cars to suppress a burgeoning pro-democracy movement that had encamped in Beijing's Tiananmen Square. Estimates on the number of demonstrators killed vary between 700 and 2,700.

June 5, 1989 in the wake of the Tiananmen Square massacres, President Bush announces a number of condemnatory actions, including the suspension of the sale of American weapons to China.

August 9, 1989 President Bush signs into law the Financial Institutions Reform, Recovery, and Enforcement Act of 1989, a compromise with Congress on the bailout of savings and loans. This law differs from Bush's February 6 proposal of financing the bailout from the Treasury Department through the sale of bonds. It offers $166 billion worth of aid to troubled savings and loans institutions and creates a new government body, the Resolution Trust Company, to oversee the merger or liquidation of troubled banks.

➢ **November 9, 1989 The Berlin Wall falls, marking the symbolic end of Communist rule in Eastern Europe.**

December 2-3, 1989 President Bush and Soviet President Mikhail Gorbachev hold their first meeting of Bush's presidency in the harbor of Valetta, Malta, to discuss nuclear disarmament and the strengthening of Soviet-American trade relations. Both leaders announce that the Cold War is effectively over.

➢ **December 20, 1989 American armed forces invade Panama to capture Manuel Antonio Noriega, the country's military dictator. Noriega, who had been indicted in the United States on drug trafficking charges, surrendered on January 3, 1990. He was convicted on drug charges on April 9, 1992, and sent to prison.**

June 1, 1990 at a summit meeting in Washington, D.C., President Bush and Soviet President Mikhail Gorbachev sign the broadest arms reduction agreement in two decades. The agreement stipulates that the United States and the Soviet Union scrap 25 percent and 40 percent of their respective nuclear stockpiles.

June 26, 1990 President Bush, in a written statement released to the press, reneges on his "no new taxes" pledge from the 1988 presidential campaign by stating that in order to solve the deficit problem, tax increases might be necessary for the 1991 fiscal year.

August 2, 1990 Iraq invades Kuwait. President Bush strongly condemns Iraq's actions, setting the stage for an American response.

October 3, 1990 Seven months after East Germans overwhelmingly approve reunification, the two German states are formally reunited.

Strangling of American Liberty

October 22, 1990 President Bush vetoes the Civil Rights Act of 1990, stating that the bill would "introduce the destructive force of quotas into our nation's employment system."

November 5, 1990 President Bush signs a budget law intended to reduce the federal budget by almost $500 billion over the next five years. The law includes $140 billion dollars in new taxes.

November 8, 1990 President Bush increases the number of American troops in Saudi Arabia to 400,000.

November 19, 1990 The United States, Canada, and twenty other European nations sign the Conventional Forces in Europe Treaty (CFE). The CFE limits NATO and Warsaw Pact weapons holdings and caps the American troop presence in Central Europe at 195,000.

> ➤ **November 29, 1990 President Bush signs the Immigration Act of 1990, the most extensive revision to immigration law in more than a half century. The new law allows for the admission of 700,000 aliens each year.**

January 17, 1991 The Persian Gulf War, code-named Operation Desert Storm, begins with a massive, American-led air attack on Iraq.

February 24, 1991 Ground troops, including a large contingent of American soldiers, begin operations in Operation Desert Storm.

February 27, 1991 after liberating Kuwait, coalition troops advance rapidly into Iraqi territory, encountering no resistance. President Bush, deciding that the war's objectives had been met, calls off the ground offensive.

July 10, 1991 President Bush lifts most American sanctions against the Republic of South Africa, saying that the movement to end apartheid is now "irreversible."

July 31, 1991 President Bush and Mikhail Gorbachev meet in Moscow to sign a nuclear arms reduction treaty (START-I) which calls for both nations to make significant reductions in the number of nuclear warheads in their respective arsenals.

October 15, 1991 Clarence Thomas, President Bush's nominee to replace retiring justice Harry A. Blackmun on the Supreme Court, is confirmed by the Senate in a close 52-48 vote. Thomas' confirmation hearings focus on charges of sexual harassment made by Anita F. Hill, a law professor and former colleague of Thomas.

November 21, 1991 President Bush signs the Civil Rights Act of 1991, making it easier for employees to sue employers on grounds of discrimination.

December 31, 1991 the constituent republics of the Soviet Union dissolve the Union of Soviet Socialist Republics.

January 10, 1992 The Labor Department announces that the unemployment rose to 7.1 percent in December 1991, the highest mark in over five years.

February 1, 1992 at the presidential retreat at Camp David, Maryland, President Bush and Russian president Boris Yeltsin meet to discuss U.S.-Russian relations and officially declare the end of the Cold War.

> ➤ **May 23, 1992 The United States signs agreements with Russia, Belarus, Ukraine, and Kazakhstan, ensuring the continued participation of these nations in the nuclear arms reduction treaties signed by the U.S.S.R. before its collapse in late 1991.**

June 16, 1992 President Bush and President Yeltsin announce an agreement by which the United States and Russia reduce their nuclear warheads to between 3,000 and 3,500 by the year 2003.

November 3, 1992

Strangling of American Liberty

Arkansas Governor Bill Clinton, a Democrat, is elected President after defeating President Bush and Ross Perot, an independent from Texas. Clinton wins 43 percent of the vote and 370 Electoral College votes, to Bush's 38 percent and 168, and Perot's 19 percent and 0.

December 9, 1992

American troops land in Somalia as part of the UN-sponsored "Operation Restore Hope." The humanitarian mission's first goal was to ensure the distribution of food and medical aid and supplies to suffering Somalis. Somalia had been wracked by starvation, drought, and violence.

January 20, 1993 William Jefferson Clinton is inaugurated as the forty-second President of the United States.

January 25, 1993 President Clinton announces that First Lady Hillary Rodham Clinton will head the Task Force on National Health Care Reform. The President hopes to reform the nation's health care system so that all Americans have health insurance, ensuring what is called "universal coverage," and to control the skyrocketing costs of health care.

> ## *Clinton turns the White House into a den of Whores*
> ## *8 Years of Corruption*

February 5, 1993 President Clinton signs the Family Medical Leave Act that requires companies to provide workers with up to three months of unpaid leave for family and medical emergencies.

➤ **February 26, 1993 .Six people are killed and more than a thousand suffer injuries after a bomb planted under the World Trade Centre in New York City explodes. The bomb marks the beginning of a string of threats against the United States made during the Clinton administration by both foreign and domestic terrorists.**

March 11, 1993 The Senate confirms Janet Reno as attorney general, the first woman to serve in the position. Reno was Clinton's third choice for the position, after his first two selections were scuttled due to financial improprieties.

➤ **April 19, 1993 In Waco, Texas, federal law enforcement officers, under the orders of Attorney General Janet Reno, end a 51-day standoff against a religious cult led by self-styled messiah David Koresh. In the ensuing confrontation, the fires that destroy the cult's compound kill at least seventy-five people, and bring Reno widespread criticism for her aggressive handling of the situation.**

June 26, 1993 The U.S. Navy, under President Clinton's orders, attacks Iraqi intelligence operations in downtown Baghdad after learning that Iraqis had plotted to kill former President Bush during his April 1993 visit to Kuwait. The twenty-three tomahawk missiles fired reportedly kill eight people.

➤ **July 19, 1993 President Clinton announces an "honourable compromise" in the debate surrounding gays in the military. Homosexuals would be allowed to serve, but could face military investigations if they acknowledged their orientation, as well as be expelled for it. The policy is labelled "Don't Ask, Don't Tell."**

Strangling of American Liberty

July 20, 1993 Vince Foster, deputy counsel to the President, is found dead in a Northern Virginia park. Authorities rule his death a suicide, but subsequent federal investigators will re-open the case in the future.

August 3, 1993 The Senate confirms Ruth Bader Ginsburg's nomination to the Supreme Court. Ginsburg succeeds the retiring Byron White and become the second woman to sit on the high court.

.

> **September 13, 1993 President Clinton presides over a ceremony in Washington, D.C., at which Israeli Prime Minister Yitzhak Rabin and PLO Chairman Yasser Arafat sign the Israeli-Palestinian Declaration of Principles, the first agreement between Jews and Palestinians, providing for Palestinian self-government in the Gaza Strip and the West Bank.**

October 3-4, 1993 an elite American special forces unit searching for Somali warlord Mohammed Farah Aidid in Somalia's capital city of Mogadishu is ambushed by Aidid's forces, leaving eighteen Americans dead. Three days later, President Clinton announces that all American military personnel in Somalia will be home by March 31, 1994.

November 30, 1993 President Clinton signs the Brady Act, which requires a potential handgun purchaser to wait five days while a background check is performed by law enforcement officers.

January 10-11, 1994 President Clinton attends the NATO summit meeting in Brussels, Belgium, at which he announces that the United States will maintain at least 100,000 troops in Europe. He also introduces the "Partnership for Peace" program aimed at building closer ties between NATO and former Warsaw Pact states.

February 3, 1994 President Clinton ends the nineteen-year old trade embargo against Vietnam, noting that Vietnam is indeed trying to locate 2,238 Americans listed as missing in action since the Vietnam War.

March 25, 1994 the last American marines leave Somalia.

May 26, 1994 President Clinton renews China's Most Favoured Nation trade status, even though China has not made as much progress on human rights issues as he had hoped.

July 25, 1994 President Clinton meets with Prime Minister Yitzhak Rabin of Israel and King Hussein of Jordan. The talks result in Israel and Jordan agreeing in principle to end nearly fifty years of official antagonism.

August 26, 1994

The White House and congressional leaders, including Senate Majority Leader George Mitchell (D-ME), announce that Clinton's ambitious plan for health care reform will not be acted upon in 1994. Clinton's initiatives fail to find support in Congress.

September 18, 1994 after a tense standoff with the Clinton administration, Haiti's military government, led by General Raoul Cedras, agrees to cede power. The administration, along with the United Nations, had tried for over a year to restore the democratically elected president of Haiti, Jean-Bertrand Aristide, who had been overthrown in a coup on September 30, 1991.

October 9, 1994 The Clinton administration announces plans to send more than 35,000 troops to the Persian Gulf to deter an Iraqi invasion of Kuwait. Less than three days after the announcement, Iraqi troops pull back from the Iraq-Kuwait border.

Strangling of American Liberty

> **November 8, 1994 in mid-term congressional elections, the Republican Party wins control of both houses of Congress for the first time in more than 40 years. It now holds a 53 to 47 advantage in the Senate and a 230 to 214 to 1 lead in the House.**

December 5, 1994 President Clinton, along with the presidents of Belarus, Kazakhstan, Russia, and Ukraine, signs the Strategic Arms Reduction Treaty (START I) in Budapest, Hungary. The treaty eliminates more than 9,000 warheads.

April 19, 1995 in an act of domestic terrorism, a bomb planted in a truck parked in front of the Alfred P. Murrah Federal Building in Oklahoma City, Oklahoma, kills 168 people and causes massive structural damage. In the days following the tragedy, Clinton, in widely praised efforts, speaks with victims and to the country about how to recover physically, emotionally, and spiritually from the attack.

July 11, 1995 The United States extended full diplomatic recognition of Vietnam, twenty-two years after the United States withdrew military forces from that country.

August 30, 1995 NATO, with a strong contingent of American forces, begins two weeks of air attacks on Serbian positions.

October 23, 1995 President Clinton and Russian president Yeltsin meet in Hyde Park, New York, and continue to discuss ways to improve relations between their two nations, especially with regard to the issue of nuclear arms.

November-December, 1995 President Clinton and the Republican-controlled Congress, led by Speaker of the House Newt Gingrich (R-GA), engage in a political death struggle over how to balance the budget by 2002. Failure to reach an agreement leads to the shutdown of certain parts of the federal government, furloughing more than a quarter of a million government workers.

November 21, 1995 In Dayton, Ohio, the representatives of Bosnia, Croatia, and Serbia agree in principle to a peace agreement, brokered by American Richard Holbrooke, to end three years of war in Bosnia. The agreement establishes a unitary Bosnian state and allows refugees to return home.

January 23, 1996

President Clinton, in the annual State of the Union address, declares, "The era of big government is over." More important, he positions himself as a centrist, moderate Democrat for the upcoming presidential election, hoping that these types of pronouncements will blunt Republican charges that he is too liberal.

April 9, 1996 President Clinton signs a bill giving him the power of the "line-item veto," which had been requested by Presidents Reagan and Bush. With this new power, Clinton can veto specific items in spending and tax bills without vetoing the entire measure.

April 10, 1996 President Clinton vetoes a bill that would have outlawed certain types of late-term abortions, namely the partial birth abortion. Clinton emerges during his presidency as a strong advocate of the "right to choose," often stating his wish that abortions in the United States become "safe, legal, and rare."

Strangling of American Liberty

April 29, 1996 Vice President Al Gore attends a Democratic National Committee fundraising event at a Buddhist temple in Los Angeles. Gore and the DNC raise more than $60,000, but so through questionable interpretations of several campaign finance laws. The Clinton administration comes under increasing criticism in its second term for these alleged violations.

May 15, 1996 President Clinton announces that American troops will likely remain in Bosnia as the major component of an international peacekeeping force for an additional eighteen months.

May 28, 1996 in the first trial to result from the White-water investigation, Jim and Susan McDougal, and Arkansas Governor Jim Guy Tucker--Clinton's friends and former business partners in the White-water affair--are convicted of fraud.

September 3, 1996 President Clinton orders a cruise missile strike against Iraq after Saddam Hussein leads a siege against the Kurdish city of Irbil in northern Iraq.

September 24, 1996 an overwhelming majority of United Nations, members, including the United States, agree to a treaty banning all nuclear weapons testing.

November 5, 1996

President Clinton, with 49 percent of the vote, defeats Senator Bob Dole (R-KS), with 41 percent of the vote, for the presidency. Clinton becomes the first Democratic President since Franklin Roosevelt to win re-election to a second term.

December 5, 1996 President Clinton selects Madeline Albright, the American ambassador to the United Nations, to serve as his secretary of state. After winning Senate confirmation, Albright is sworn in on January 23, 1997, becoming the first women to hold the position.

➤ **March 11, 1997 The Senate votes 99-0 to approve an investigation into the "improper" and "illegal" fund-raising tactics of both the White House and members of Congress. Allegations by Republicans and some Democrats of illegal fund raising by the Clinton White House spur the investigation.**

March 21, 1997 President Clinton and President Yeltsin of Russia meet at Helsinki, Finland, and agree to begin negotiations on another nuclear arms reduction treaty (START III) as soon as both nations ratify START II. The United States Senate had ratified START II in January 1996.

➤ **May 27, 1997 in a decision affecting both the scope of presidential power and the immediate future of the Clinton presidency, the Supreme Court rules that Paula Jones can pursue her sexual harassment lawsuit against President Clinton, even while he is in office.**

October 3, 1997 Attorney General Janet Reno, in a letter to Congress, announces that the Justice Department's investigation into allegations that the Clinton administration violated campaign finance laws, especially in its efforts to finance the 1996 presidential campaign, has uncovered no major violations.

October 31, 1997 President Clinton orders the United States government to contribute $3 billion to an international bailout of Indonesia totalling over $22 billion. The Clinton administration argues that the bailout will help stabilize the shaky financial situation in Southeast Asia.

Strangling of American Liberty

- January 20, 1998 Newsbreaks that President Clinton may have had a sexual relationship with a former White House intern named Monica Lewinsky. Clinton, adamantly denying the allegations, states, "I did not have sexual relations with that woman, Miss Lewinsky."

- April 2, 1998 a judge dismisses Paula Jones's sexual harassment lawsuit against President Clinton.

- August 7, 1998 Terrorists bomb American embassies in Kenya and Tanzania, killing 224 people, including 20 Americans. United States intelligence believes that Osama bin Laden, a Saudi exile and alleged terrorist leader, is behind the attacks. On August 20, the U.S. military, on orders from President Clinton, launch reprisal strikes on "terrorist related facilities" in Afghanistan, bin Laden's country of residence, and Sudan. The attacks on Sudan, however, come under particular scrutiny, as a number of international observers and members of the Sudanese government contend that the United States destroyed a civilian pharmaceutical facility, and not a chemical weapons plant, as the Clinton administration reported.

- September 11, 1998 The Office of the Independent Counsel releases its report on the Clinton-Lewinsky affair, commonly known as the Starr Report. Two days earlier, Independent Counsel Kenneth Starr tells the House that he has uncovered information that may be grounds for impeachment.

October 23, 1998 after nine days of negotiations in rural Maryland, Israeli leader Benjamin Netanyahu and Palestinian leader Yasser Arafat sign the Wye River Memorandum. President Clinton mediates the negotiations, which result in an agreement highlighted by a three-stage withdrawal of Israeli troops from the West Bank.

> **December 16, 1998 President Clinton orders a three-day bombing attack against Iraq after Saddam Hussein refuses to cooperate with United Nations weapons inspectors.**

> **December 19, 1998 The House of Representatives votes to impeach President Clinton on charges of perjury and obstruction of justice.**

❖ January 20, 1999 President Clinton delivers his State of the Union address to a joint session of Congress under remarkable circumstances: six days earlier, the Senate had convened an impeachment trial against the President. Despite the impeachment process, public opinion polls show Clinton with his highest approval ratings.

❖ February 12, 1999 The Senate acquits President Clinton on both articles of impeachment, rejecting one article and splitting evenly on the second.

March 24, 1999 in response to Serbian aggression in Kosovo and Albania, and reports of ethnic cleansing, the United States leads NATO attacks against Serbia. On February 23, Serbian and Kosovar representatives had agreed to a plan that would have granted more autonomy to Kosovo over a three-year period. Serbia reneged on the agreement, prompting U.S. and NATO military action.

Strangling of American Liberty

June 10, 1999 The NATO air campaign against Serbia ends after Serb forces agree on June 9 to withdraw from Kosovo. KFOR, an international peacekeeping force of 50,000 troops, enforces the agreement.

June 3-5, 2000

President Clinton holds his first summit meeting with Russian president Vladimir Putin. They reaffirm their nations' commitment to strategic arms reductions, but disagree over American plans to research and develop a missile-defence system.

July 11-26, 2000 President Clinton hosts Israeli leader Ehud Barak and Palestinian leader Yasser Arafat at Camp David in the hope of reaching a peace agreement. After two weeks of unsuccessful talks, the summit breaks up with no agreement.

August 14, 2000 President Clinton speaks at the opening day of the Democratic National Convention. Vice President Al Gore wins the Democratic nomination for President. His challenger is Republican governor George W. Bush of Texas.

> **September 20, 2000 Independent Counsel Robert Ray announces that his investigation has not discovered enough evidence to indict the Clintons for their White-water dealings.**

October 7, 2000 In Serbia, President Slobodan Milosevic declares that Vojislav Kostunica is the rightful president of Serbia. The announcement comes after disputed elections, which Milosevic had tried to rig, produce massive street protests.

November 7, 2000 on Election Day, Vice President Gore and Governor Bush run so closely that no winner can be declared. Only after the Supreme Court rules on December 13 that there would be no recount of Florida's contested votes does Gore concede the election to Bush.

The Election was decided by the Supreme Court

The Democrats were angry and for the next eight years the media stayed on George W. Bush

January 20, 2001Texas governor George W. Bush is inaugurated as the forty-third President of the United States.

> *November 7, 2000 Americans votes in the 2000 presidential election. Vote differentials in several states are exceedingly close, with the Democratic and Republican candidates disputing many of those counts, leaving the final result inconclusive.*

> *December 12, 2000 in a 5-4 ruling, the U.S. Supreme Court stops the recount of votes in several contested Florida counties. The Democratic candidate, Vice President Albert Gore Jr., concedes the election, leaving Governor George W. Bush of Texas, the Republican candidate, as President-elect.*

January 20, 2001 George W. Bush is inaugurated as the 43rd President of the United States. He is the second son of a President to occupy the Oval Office, the first being John Quincy Adams in 1825.

January 22, 2001 in one of his first policy decisions, President Bush decides to reinstate the ban on aid to international groups performing or counselling on abortion. The ban was initiated by former President Ronald Reagan but is not enforced during the administration of President Bill Clinton.

Strangling of American Liberty

January 29, 2001 by executive order, President Bush creates the Office of Faith-Based and Community Initiatives. The new office will work to ease regulations on religious charities and promote grass-roots efforts to tackle community issues such as aid to the poor and disadvantaged.

February 16, 2001 United States airplanes attack Iraqi radar sites to enforce a "no-fly zone." Bush calls the military action a "routine mission."

March 29, 2001 The Bush administration affirms its decision to abandon ratification of the Kyoto Protocol, an international treaty signed by 180 countries to reduce global warming that set limits on industrial emissions.

April 1, 2001 A U.S. spy plane flying over the South China Sea is clipped by a Chinese fighter jet, forcing the American plane to make an emergency landing on Chinese soil. The incident strains diplomatic ties between the two nations as the United States demands that China return both the plane and its crew to American authorities.

> ➤ **April 4, 2001The Miami Herald and USA Today release a comprehensive review of the 2000 presidential election recount efforts in Florida. The review shows that even if Democratic candidate Al Gore had succeeded in getting the recounts he wanted, President Bush would have won Florida by 1,665 votes.**

April 25, 2001 President Bush signals a change in relations with China by officially pledging military support for Taiwan in the event of an attack by China. This is the first time a presidential administration has publicly acknowledged a position that had previously been implicitly accepted.

June 7, 2001 President Bush signs a $1.35 trillion tax cut into law. Although the amount falls short of the $1.60 trillion the administration has been seeking, the bill does slash income tax rates across the board and provides for the gradual elimination of the estate tax.

August 9, 2001 President Bush addresses the nation, outlining his plans for the federal funding of stem cell research. The new policy allows for government funding of research on already extracted stem cells but prohibits the extraction of additional stem cells from human embryos.

❖ *September 11, 2001 Terrorists hijack four commercial jets and crash them into the World Trade Center in New York City, the Pentagon in Washington, D.C., and the Pennsylvania countryside. It Is the worst attack on American soil since Pearl Harbor, with fatalities numbering about 3,000. Addressing the nation twelve hours after the attacks, President Bush vows to hunt down those responsible.*

> *The greatest disaster to hit the US happen on*
> *September 11, 2001*
> *Our Country was facing a threat from a group of*
> *people who had started a Holy War*
> *Islam was at war with the USA*

Strangling of American Liberty

September 20, 2001 President Bush appears before a joint session of Congress to outline the administration's lans to defeat world terrorism, singling out Osama bin Laden and his al-Qaeda organization as the primary targets of such a policy. He states that every nation must take sides in the international conflict against worldwide terrorist networks; he also warns Americans to prepare for a protracted campaign against terrorism. The President then appoints Pennsylvania governor Tom Ridge to the new cabinet-level post of director of the Office of Homeland Security. Governor Ridge will coordinate the efforts of more than forty federal agencies to secure the United States against future terrorist attacks.

October 7, 2001 speaking from the Treaty Room of the White House, President Bush announces the commencement of military action in Afghanistan; an operation code-named "Enduring Freedom."

October 17, 2001 The Capital shuts down amidst an Anthrax scare. Persons in Florida and New York have already tested positive for the frequently fatal bacteria. Bush calls for $1.5 billion to fight bioterrorism.

December 2, 2001 The Enron Corporation files for Chapter 11 bankruptcy protection, the largest bankruptcy case in American history. The beleaguered company, once the world's premier energy trading and services firm, files for court protection after watching its stock price plummet as a result of accounting issues relating to its operations. Earlier in the year, discoveries reveal that Enron's chief financial officer engaged in partnerships which allowed the company to hide half a billion dollars' worth of debt. The Bush administration has ties to key Enron executives, including CEO Kenneth Lay, but denies any involvement in the scandal.

December 13, 2001 after conferring with the National Security Council, President Bush notifies Russia of his intention to withdraw from the 1972 Anti-Ballistic Missile Treaty. Meetings with Russian president Vladimir Putin fail to establish an agreement between the two nations. In June 2002, the United States officially withdraws from the Treaty, allowing it to conduct anti-missile defence tests.

January 8, 2002 President Bush signs a landmark education reform bill into law known as the No Child Left behind Act, it offers local authorities greater flexibility in spending federal dollars, but requires standardized math and reading tests.

> *January 29, 2002 in his State of the Union address, President Bush warns that the war against terrorism is only beginning. Specifically citing North Korea, Iran, and Iraq, Bush speaks of "an axis of evil" threatening world peace.*

April 4, 2002 Secretary of State Colin Powell travels to the Middle East for talks with Israel and Palestinian leader Yasser Arafat.

> *March 22, 2002 Bush renews his call on Palestinian leader Yasser Arafat to end attacks on Israel, indicating that a meeting with Vice President Dick Cheney could still take place if Arafat yielded to American demands. Cheney, on a trip to the Middle East, refuses to meet with Arafat in the current environment. Meanwhile, Arafat remains penned in Ramallah by Israeli threats since December. On March 29, Israeli troops will take over most of his headquarters.*

Strangling of American Liberty

> *May 12, 2002 Former President Jimmy Carter travels to Cuba for a tour and visit with Cuban President Fidel Castro. His arrival marks the first trip by an American President in forty years. On May 20, President Bush announces that the forty-year-old trade embargo against Cuba will continue until conditions, including free and fair elections, are met.*

May 16, 2002 Congress presses the Bush administration for further information about warnings of the September 11, 2001, attacks. National Security Advisor Condoleezza Rice holds a briefing, maintaining, "I don't think that anybody could have predicted that these people would take an airplane and slam it into the World Trade Center, take another one and slam it into the Pentagon." She insists that there was no lapse in intelligence.

May 24, 2002 At the Kremlin, President Bush and Russian president Vladimir Putin sign a nuclear arms treaty, vowing to reduce their nations' arsenals by two-thirds over the next ten years.

June 6, 2002 in a televised address to the nation, President Bush announces broad changes to security departments in charge of protecting the nation from terrorism. The Office of Homeland Security will now coordinate a wide range of functions and oversee more than 100 organizations. The announcement follows criticism of the FBI and CIA for failing to prevent the September 11 attacks.

> *June 24, 2002 President Bush calls for the Palestinian people to replace Yasser Arafat, head of the Palestinian Authority and leader of the Palestinian cause for more than thirty years. Bush states, "When the Palestinians have new leaders, institutions and security arrangements, the U.S. will support the creation of a Palestinian state."*

July 8, 2002 Following the Enron and WorldCom scandals, in which both companies claimed profits, which turned out to be highly inflated; President Bush calls for new laws on corporate abuse. On July 10, the Dow Jones index drops below 9,000, its largest one-day loss since September 2001.

> ➤ *September 4, 2002 seeking support for action against Iraq, President Bush addresses Congress, identifying Iraqi strongman Saddam Hussein as "a serious threat." Bush mentions the concept of a regime change and announces the visit of British Prime Minister Tony Blair in the days to come. House Majority Whip Tom DeLay (R-TX) calls action in Iraq "inevitable."*

> ➤ *September 12, 2002 President Bush addresses the United Nations' Security Council, making his case for military action to enforce UN resolutions in Iraq. Additionally, he warns that the United States will move alone if the Council does not act. In the coming days, Bush and Secretary of State Colin Powell will continue to press the Security Council for a resolution against Iraq. France, Germany, and Russia, all permanent members of the Security Council, express severe reservations.*

> ➤ *October 10, 2002 a bipartisan Senate vote of 77-23 gives authorization to Bush to use force against Iraq. The Senate vote follows a similar vote of 296-133 in the House in support of the bill.*

November 5, 2002

In a sweeping mid-term election victory, Republicans gain control of the Senate and maintain their edge in the House.

After months of discussions and with Senate and Congress approval, the war begins in Iraq. This decision will become Bush's down fall.

This is one of the most important votes of the Congress and Senate. This will be used against Bush in the coming years.

December 20, 2002 Following a United Nations report issued by arms inspectors indicating that Iraq remained in violation of Security Council Resolution 1441, Bush speaks out again against Iraq. Inspections in Iraq continue.

January 7, 2003 Bush reveals a tax-cut plan of $674 billion over ten years. He suggests that the plan will stimulate the U.S. economy, end the recession, and create jobs. Democrats dismiss the plan as financially irresponsible and favourable to the rich.

February 1, 2003 the seven-member crew of the shuttle, Columbia dies in an explosion in space. Debris falls in Texas.

February 12, 2003 CIA director George Tenet announces that North Korea possesses a nuclear ballistic missile capable of hitting the United States. In the following weeks, reports emerge which suggest that North Korea will soon possess the ability to create a nuclear arsenal.

- **March 16, 2003** after months of debate in the United Nations Security Council, President Bush announces the U.S. intention to move against Iraq with its coalition of allies. Bush issues an ultimatum for military action, giving Iraqi leader Saddam Hussein and his sons forty-eight hours to leave Iraq.

- **March 19, 2003** the 8:00 p.m. deadline for Hussein to leave Iraq passes. At 10:15 p.m., Bush addresses the nation and informs the American people that the United States is at war with Iraq.

- **March 25, 2003** citing costs of the Iraq War, the Senate approves, by a vote of 51-48, the reduction of Bush's tax cut plan to $350 million, less than half of the original amount.

- **April 10, 2003** President Bush and British Prime Minister Tony Blair air a joint address on Iraqi television that describes the goals of coalition forces and reassures the Iraqi people that they will be able to live their lives in peace and security in a post-Saddam era.

- **May 1, 2003** in a nationally televised address aboard the aircraft carrier *USS Abraham Lincoln*, Bush stands in front of a "Mission Accomplished" banner and declares that major combat operations in Iraq are over. He links the Iraq War to the War on Terror and vows to continue searching for banned weapons in Iraq.

May 22, 2003 The UN Security Council votes to lift sanctions on Iraq imposed since the 1991 Gulf War. The resolution gives the United States and United Kingdom control of Iraq until it establishes a legitimate government and authority to use Iraqi oil revenues for humanitarian aid and reconstruction.

Strangling of American Liberty

May 28, 2003 Bush signs into law his $350 billion tax-cut package, the third largest in history, in an effort to strengthen the U.S. economy and reverse a trend of increasing unemployment. Congressional Democrats who opposed the bill argued it is skewed towards the wealthy.

June 4, 2003 Bush meets with Israeli Prime Minister Ariel Sharon and Palestinian Prime Minister Mahmoud Abbas in Aqaba, Jordan, to discuss implementation of a "road-map" for peace.

June 17, 2003 President Bush issues comprehensive guidelines forbidding federal law enforcement agencies from considering race or ethnicity in routine patrol duties. Although more extensive than previous federal law, the guidelines provided clear exceptions for matters of national security and counterterrorism operations.

July 11, 2003 CIA Director George Tenet accepts full responsibility for the statement in Bush's 2003 State of the Union Address regarding Iraq's alleged effort to obtain uranium from Africa, saying its inclusion should not have been approved by the CIA because the intelligence was unsubstantiated and the claim had been discredited.

> *July 22, 2003 U.S. forces kill Saddam Hussein's two sons Uday and Qusay in Mosul, Iraq. Officials hope that anti-U.S. attacks in Iraq will decrease as a result. Saddam Hussein's whereabouts are unknown.*

July 24, 2003 the joint Congressional Committee on Intelligence releases an 800-page document on the findings of its inquiry into intelligence failures leading up to the terrorist attacks of September 11, which concludes that intelligence agencies failed to respond to alerts about potential targets and methods. The report faults the NSA, CIA, and the FBI for a breakdown in communications and advocates the creation of a cabinet-level "intelligence czar" to remove obstacles between agencies.

September 30, 2003 The Justice Department announces a full criminal investigation into allegations that Bush administration officials had leaked the name of a covert CIA operative to the media in July. Bush urges full cooperation with the probe.

October 2, 2003 Chief U.S. Weapons Inspector David Kay reports that his 1,400-member team, the Iraq Survey Group, failed to find any biological, chemical, or nuclear weapons in Iraq. Kay acknowledged that they did find evidence that Iraq sought the capacity to create those weapons in the future. Bush used these findings as validation of his pre-war claims that Iraq posed a significant security threat to the United States.

November 5, 2003 Bush signs into law a ban on late-term abortion, the first law to ban an abortion procedure since the Supreme Court's 1973 decision in *Roe v. Wade*. The Supreme Court later upholds the ban.

December 8, 2003 Bush signs a landmark bill overhauling Medicare that includes the program's first prescription drug benefits to begin in 2006 and creates incentives for private insurance companies to cover Medicare subscribers.

> ➤ *December 18, 2003 Iran signs an agreement to grant unrestricted access to UN-IAEA weapons inspectors.*

January 20, 2004 Bush gives his fourth State of the Union Address, laying out a broad domestic and foreign policy agenda while stressing issues of national security.

March 8, 2004 The Iraqi Governing Council signs an interim constitution to provide a framework for establishment of a transitional government.

Strangling of American Liberty

> *April 4, 2004 U.S. forces in Iraq confront a violent uprising beginning with Shiite Muslims in Baghdad and spreading to Sunni guerrillas in Fallujah, leading to the heaviest fighting since the invasion began in March of 2003.*

April 28, 2004 CBS broadcasts photographs of U.S. Army abuse of Iraqi prisoners in Abu Ghraib prison, a facility on the outskirts of Baghdad. Bush and other senior administration officials voice deep disapproval over these abuses.

> ❖ *May 17, 2004 Massachusetts becomes the first state to offer marriage licenses to same sex couples. Bush reiterates to Congress his call for a constitutional amendment banning same sex marriage.*

June 3, 2004 Bush announces he has accepted the resignation of CIA Director George Tenet, widely blamed for intelligence failures in the months leading up to September 11.

June 8, 2004 Attorney General John Ashcroft appears before the Senate Judiciary Committee to answer questions regarding two leaked government memoranda that contained legal arguments for circumventing U.S. and international bans on torture, specifically for the questioning of terrorist suspects.

> ➢ *June 28, 2004 The U.S.-led Coalition for Provisional Authority formerly ends foreign occupation of Iraq, granting the provisional government sovereignty. Still, 130,000 troops remain in Iraq.*

September 2, 2004 resident Bush and Vice President Cheney are renominated as the Republican candidates at the GOP convention in New York City.

❖ *September 30, 2004 Bush and Democratic nominee, Senator John Kerry, have their first of three presidential debates, this one focused on national security issues and foreign policy. The Bush administration's handling of the Iraq War is the main focus.*

October 29, 2004 Qatar-based television channel Al-Jazeera airs excerpts from a videotape of Osama bin-Laden, leader of the terrorist network al-Qaeda, who addresses the American people. Many view this tape as an attempt by al-Qaeda to influence the U.S. presidential election.

November 3, 2004 Bush wins a second term with 51 percent of the popular vote and 274 electoral votes to John Kerry's 252. The Republican Party builds slightly on its majority in the House and Senate.

November 8, 2004 U.S. troops launch an assault to retake the rebel-controlled city of Fallujah in the largest military operation since the initial invasion in March of 2003.

November 15, 2004 Retired Army general and Secretary of State Colin Powell resigns. Bush appoints former National Security Advisor Condoleezza Rice to the position.

January 20, 2005 President Bush is sworn in for the second term of his presidency.

February 2, 2005 in his State of the Union, President Bush calls for an historic restructuring of Social Security, allowing workers to use their payroll taxes to invest in the stock market. However, he is unable to move the policy through Congress.

Strangling of American Liberty

February 17, 2005 Bush names former U.S. Ambassador to Iraq John Negroponte Director of National Intelligence, a newly created position of "intelligence czar" created in the wake of Congressional investigations into intelligence failures leading up to September 11.

February 20-24, 2005 Bush travels to Europe to meet with French President Jacques Chirac, German Chancellor Gerhard Schroeder, and Russian President Vladimir Putin to smooth diplomatic relations after the U.S.-led invasion of Iraq.

March 31, 2005 Terri Schiavo, a Florida woman long-suffering from brain damage, dies following the removal of her feeding tube. Schiavo had been the focus of legal controversy between the wishes of her parents and those of her husband. Ten days earlier, President Bush had signed a law permitting Schiavo's parents to challenge the removal of her feeding tube in federal court.

June 5, 2005 Iraqi government announces that a war crimes trial for Saddam Hussein is likely to begin within the next two months and prosecutors would seek the death penalty.

June 10, 2005 South Korean President Roh Moo Hyun meets with Bush to discuss efforts to persuade North Korea to join the six-party talks intended to end North Korea's pursuit of nuclear weapons.

June 21, 2005 Vietnamese Premier Phan Van Khai meets with Bush to discuss human rights and treatment of ethnic and religious minorities in Vietnam. This marks the first visit by a Vietnamese Premier to the United States since the country reunited under Communist rule in 1975.

June 28, 2005 The Senate easily passes an omnibus energy bill aimed at supporting the traditional energy industries of oil and natural gas, but also provides tax incentives for the use of alternative energy sources such as solar and wind power.

July 26, 2005 the space shuttle Discovery takes off from the Kennedy Space Center on a mission to deliver repairs to the International Space Station. This is the first U.S. space mission since the failed return of the Columbia in 2003.

> ➤ **August 28, 2005** Hurricane Katrina strikes the southern coast of the United States with devastating effects. The storm breaches the levee system in New Orleans, causing massive flooding and destruction of property. The Bush administration is harshly criticized for an inadequate response by the federal government to the storm's destruction.

September 29, 2005 John G. Roberts is confirmed as Chief Justice of the U.S. Supreme Court. Roberts replaces William Rehnquist, who died in office, and is President Bush's first nominee to the Court.

January 26, 2006 The Senate Judiciary Committee approves President Bush's nomination of Samuel A. Alito, Jr., to the U.S. Supreme Court by a vote of 10-8. Previously, concerns were voiced over the disruption of the court's ideological balance that would result from Alito's replacement of moderate Sandra Day O'Connor.

March 21, 2006 In a White House news conference, President Bush admits for the first time that the complete removal of U.S. troops from Iraq during the remainder of his term is improbable. He continues to assert the fact that progress is being made in the establishment of Iraqi democracy.

May 3, 2006 after several cases of avian influenza are reported in Central and Southeast Asia, the Bush administration proposes a plan to minimize losses in the case of a deadly pandemic. The plan includes coordination with the World Health Organization, reorganization of international travel, and the authorization of military assistance in the case of public unrest.

Strangling of American Liberty

- **May 4, 2006** The U.S. District Court in Alexandria, Virginia, sentences Zacarias Moussaoui to life in prison without parole for his role in the September 11, 2001, terrorist attacks. Moussaoui was the first person to stand trial for the attacks.

June 7, 2006 The Senate votes 49-48 to conclude debate on a constitutional amendment banning same sex marriages in the United States, thereby preventing a vote on the actual passage of the amendment. President Bush had previously expressed support of the proposed amendment.

July 19, 2006 President Bush vetoes a bill to lift constraints on federal funding of embryonic stem cell research, and subsequently, the House unsuccessfully attempts to override the veto. This is the first veto Bush issues during his administration.

October 26, 2006 President Bush signs a bill providing for the construction of a 700-mile fence along the United States-Mexico border, in an effort to increase border security and stem illegal immigration.

November 7, 2006 Democrats recapture control of the U.S. House and Senate in the midterm elections.

- **December 30, 2006** Former Iraqi President Saddam Hussein is hanged in Baghdad, Iraq, after being convicted of crimes against humanity dating back to 1982.

- **January 4, 2007** Nancy Pelosi, a Democrat from California, takes office as the first female Speaker of the House. Democrats assume control of both the House of Representatives and the Senate.

January 8, 2007 The U.S. Air Force launches an air attack on Islamist militias and suspected al-Qaeda operatives in Somalia.

January 11, 2007 Bush announces what would be termed a "troop surge" in Iraq in an attempt to increase security in the capital of Baghdad and smother insurgency centers throughout the country.

February 10, 2007 General David Petraeus takes over command of the multinational forces in Iraq to oversee the surge.

March 6, 2007 Scooter Libby, Vice President Cheney's chief of staff, is convicted of perjury and obstruction of justice in the case of CIA operative, Valerie Plame Wilson, whose covert identity was exposed. President Bush later commutes Libby's sentence.

April 16, 2007 Seung-Hui Cho kills himself and 32 fellow students at Virginia Tech in the deadliest campus gun rampage in U.S. history. President Bush and the First Lady attend the memorial.

May 1, 2007 Bush vetoes a war-spending bill passed by Congress, which set a timetable for troop withdrawal from Iraq. Within days, Bush reaches a record low approval rating.

June 29, 2007 The Supreme Court reverses an April decision and agrees to hear appeals from Guantanamo Bay detainees who have not had access to the federal courts.

July 26, 2007 Congress passes the Antiterrorism Bill, which will allow for the screening of air and sea cargo and will give more money in government antiterrorism grants to states with the greatest risk for terrorist attacks.

September 17, 2007 President Bush names Michael Mukasey as Attorney General after Alberto Gonzalez announces his resignation.

October 9, 2007 The Dow Jones industrial average closes at 14,164, its all-time high. Soon after, it begins a steep decline.

Strangling of American Liberty

November 27, 2007 President Bush hosts a Middle East Peace Conference in Annapolis, Maryland, with Prime Minister Ehud Olmert of Israel and Palestinian president Mahmoud Abbas.

December 19, 2007 Congress passes new energy legislation to increase automobile fuel efficiency standards and mandates increases in biofuel production. The bill passes the House and Senate, and President Bush signs it into law.

January 18, 2008 President Bush proposes a $145 billion stimulus package in response to a housing crisis and rapidly increasing oil prices. The package gives individuals several hundred dollars to facilitate spending, as well as rebates for children and tax deductions for businesses in order to jump-start the slowing economy.

January 31, 2008 U.S. missile strikes in Pakistan kill a top al-Qaeda leader, Abu Laith al-Libi, who trained terror operatives in the region.

February 1, 2008 The Bureau of Labour Statistics reports that the U.S. economy lost more than 15,000 jobs during the previous month. Such an elimination of jobs from the economy had not occurred for more than four years.

February 7, 2008 The Senate passes a $170-billion stimulus package to give many Americans tax rebates as large as $600 or more, and to implement tax breaks for certain businesses in an effort to head-off impending economic slowdown.

February 11, 2008 six detainees at Guantanamo Bay who were thought to have had roles in orchestrating the September 11 terrorist attacks are charged with conspiracy, murder in violation of the law of war, terrorism, and other charges. All six face the death penalty in military tribunals.

March 23, 2008 after a roadside bomb exploded in Baghdad, the U.S. death toll for the war in Iraq reached 4,000.

❖ **May 9, 2008** The State Department renews a deal with Blackwater Worldwide, the private defence contractor whose guards killed 17 civilians in 2007, to provide defence for U.S. diplomats in the Middle East.

May 22, 2008 The House and Senate override President Bush's veto of the Farm Bill, a $307 billion bill that will provide subsidies to farmers. More than $10 billion of the funds will go to expanding nutritional programs such as food stamps. Bush originally vetoed the bill, which he felt to be excessive.

June 3, 2008 Democratic candidate Barack Obama secures the party's nomination for the presidency.

❖ **June 5, 2008** The Senate Select Committee on Intelligence finds, after a five-year study, that President Bush and other officials greatly exaggerated the evidence showing that Saddam Hussein held weapons of mass destruction.

June 30, 2008 in a new report issued on the situation in Iraq, the U.S. Army admits that while it was able to adequately topple Hussein's regime, it did not have the capability to rebuild Iraq into a fully functioning new country.

➤ **September 1, 2008** U.S. forces hand over control of Anbar Province to the Iraqi military and police, who will now be responsible for maintaining order there.

September 7, 2008 The U.S. government places Fannie Mae and Freddie Mac under its control to prevent the institutions from going under and endangering more than half of the country's mortgages.

Strangling of American Liberty

October 1, 2008 Senate approves an end to the long-standing ban on trading nuclear fuels with India, who will be able to purchase fuel on the market as long as it is for civilian purposes.

October 3, 2008 at the onset of financial crisis, President Bush signs a $700 billion bailout plan for failing bank assets, the largest in U.S. history.

October 30, 2008 U.S. gross domestic product drops by 0.3 percent, the first time GDP has shrunk in 17 years.

October 31, 2008 General David Petraeus takes over as Head of Central Command, overseeing all U.S. military operations in Iraq, Afghanistan, Pakistan, Syria, and Iran.

November 4, 2008 Barack Obama is elected the next President of the United States in an historic election in which Democrats win in several traditionally Republican states and pick up seats in the House and Senate. Obama is the first African American elected President.

November 25, 2008 The Treasury Department and the Federal Reserve agree to provide another $800 billion in lending programs to buy debt insured by Fannie Mae and Freddie Mac and to provide more small loans to consumers.

For the first time in our history, a Black man is elected as President of the United States. His credentials are questioned and birth is questioned as to his heritage. He will lead the nation away from its roots. The nation will be more divided then it has ever been. He was elected with a landslide and he will abuse his power.

December 16, 2008 Federal Reserve cuts interest rates to an all-time low of zero percent, down from 1 percent and 0.25 percent earlier in the year as part of a plan to stimulate the economy.

December 19, 2008 President Bush issues a $17.4-billion auto bailout to General Motors and Chrysler to keep the two American automotive giants from going bankrupt.

January 20, 2009 Barack Obama is inaugurated the 44th President of the United States. President Bush leaves Washington, D.C., and settles in Dallas, Texas. As we look back over the events of the previous almost six decades, we can see why the country was ripe for a leader to take it in a new direction. Obama was the man the country decided to elect. The promises he made and his ability to speak drew the younger crowd. To Black America he was the hope of Martin Luther King and the county was ripe for the picking. Every failure we had made he brought up on the stump. His constant attack on the Bush years and never-ending promises drew the crowds. His promise to end the wars, and make everyone wealthy appealed to the unemployment and lazy group of people. Even the rich and famous loved him and being he was half-white and half-Black surely he would pull everyone together. Individuals who knew what the American people wanted groomed him and they were ready to give it to them. His involvement with Reverend Wright and the "Nation of Islam" was overlooked and his hatred of the White man was totally overlooked. He came into office with a plan and he has carried it out. His ability to lie and get away with it goes beyond the years of Clinton. Most Americans believed him when he said, "He was a Christian" and was able to hide his Islamic belief. Even today, people cannot see whom he is catering too. Under all reasoning if, he was a White man he would have been shot by now. The liberal media continues to support him while attacking anyone who speaks against him.

2 Thessalonians 2:11 (KJV)
[11] And for this cause God shall send them strong delusion, that they should believe a lie:

Strangling of American Liberty

People seem blinded as if they cannot see the truth.

In Chapter 7 we will talk more about Obama.

Chapter 4

Immigration

Now we need to look at Obama action on immigration.

[12]The following article: WASHINGTON — President Barack Obama's **executive order on immigration** will allow people who've been working in the country without documents to retroactively file tax returns for the past three years and collectively get about $1.7 billion in refundable tax credits over 10 years.

It is a little known consequence of the executive order on immigration announced shortly before Thanksgiving, and whose implementation is presently held up in the courts.

Republican lawmakers are scrambling to pass legislation that would limit the ability of the workers to file tax returns for years before their immigration status changed under the executive order and qualify for a tax refund that on average for other taxpayers has been about $2,300 per person.

Under Obama's executive order, eligible workers would be given Social Security numbers, and that would allow them to work legally while the order is in effect. They could file a 1040 tax return or amended returns for three years prior – the statute of limitations for amending a tax return – and potentially qualify for the refundable Earned Income Tax Credit.

"Those who were working illegally in the United States shouldn't be rewarded for doing so," Sen. Charles

---

[12] http://www.centredaily.com/2015/03/04/4632680/obama-order-could-mean-refund.html#storylink=cpy

Strangling of American Liberty

Grassley, R-Iowa, said in a statement to McClatchy. "That would have the effect of allowing retroactive benefits. My proposal would prohibit those granted deferred action from claiming the EITC for any year they were working without authorization in the United States." McClatchy obtained an estimate by the congressional Joint Committee on Taxation, done for Grassley and Senate Finance Committee Chairman Orrin Hatch, R-Utah. It shows the additional EITC refunds under the program could cost taxpayers $1.7 billion over 10 years, almost all of it in the first five years.

Obama's immigration order overall is actually expected to bring in almost $20 billion in new revenue over a 10-year period after implementation, according to the nonpartisan Congressional Budget Office. That is because new immigrants would be paying into Social Security and having taxes withheld from paychecks.

Repealing the order would add to projected deficits. However, allowing previously undocumented workers to quickly collect a government check for a time when they were not here legally is hardly a good optic for Obama and Democrats.

The Earned Income Tax Credit was created to help move individuals off welfare rolls and into employment. It provides a tax benefit to low-income earners based on what they actually earn. It is "refundable," meaning workers who have no federal income tax liabilities get the balance of the credit in a check from the government.

Allowing the new immigrants to apply retroactively for the EITC is similar to green card holders being able to seek the credit when they get a Social Security number, as is the case now.

The Internal Revenue Service recently reviewed guidance dating to 2000 and upheld that the determining factor on getting the Earned Income Tax Credit refund is a Social Security number, not immigration status.

The executive action will have two key components:

1. It would offer a legal reprieve to the undocumented parents of U.S. citizens and permanent residents who have resided in the country for at least five years. This would remove the constant threat of deportation. Many could also receive work permits.

2. It would expand the 2012 Deferred Action for Childhood Arrivals (DACA) program that allowed young immigrants, less than 30 years old, who arrived as children to apply for a deportation deferral and who are now here legally. Immigrants older than 30 now qualify, as do recent arrivals.

People in both groups will have to reapply every three years. The executive action will also include:

- A program to facilitate visas for people who invest in the United States and those who pursue science, technology, engineering and math degrees

- Modifying federal immigrant detention procedures

- Adding resources to strengthen security at the border

   Nevertheless, notably, the action will not:

- Extend protections to hundreds of thousands of parents of young immigrants who participated in the DACA program -- a group totaling 671,000 people.

- Expand visas for migrant farm workers. According to The Times, "farm workers, for example, will not be singled out for protections because of concerns that it was difficult to justify legally treating them differently from undocumented workers in other jobs, like hotel clerks, day laborers and construction workers."

- Expand the existing H-1B visa program for highly skilled foreigners

How far can a man reach? My understanding, "Obama told the public he could not use his executive privilege over twenty times to do this, yet he has and he feels no guilt about it." Once again, our liberty is at stake and the people are to stand back and do nothing about it. There is more behind this then the public understands. Allowing all of these immigrants' in to America will only build the Democratic Party. Obama has his cronies like Al Sharpton and Byron Allen who speak out of both sides of the mouth.

I have a daughter-in-law from the Ukraine who went through the full process of becoming a US citizen. It was not easy and it did cost money, but it was not made to be easy for it should be a privilege to become a citizen of the greatest country in the world. We travel all over this country and I do not think we have visited an area we did not see illegal aliens. They are working in the fields, restaurants, construction jobs and most any job a Black or White man will not work. They are not lazy and are hard workers. To be very honest, I believe they are planning on staying.

Sources have estimated America has over eleven million illegal immigrants here in the states. I believe we have many more than that. Russians, Chinese, Indonesians, Mexicans, Ukrainians, and many others have come illegally and are staying. Our borders are wide open and everyday many are coming in. Arab countries are sending people in every day who want to destroy America. The United States is no more than a melting pot of every nation who wants to get rid of the people they cannot feed. The

US is in a quandary of this issue. What do you do with people who have no birth control, having babies out of wedlock, and are in continuing need of welfare benefits?

Immigration is out of control

[13]Illegal alien migration into the United States costs American taxpayers $346 billion annually reported by the National Research Council. While employers of illegal aliens rake-in billions of dollars, the US citizens subsidize what may be called organized "Slavery in 21st Century America."

While Congress facilitates outsourcing, insourcing and offshoring of American jobs by the thousands weekly, that same Congress imports 182,000 legal immigrant monthly who need jobs. Another estimated 100,000 illegal aliens arrive each month without jobs. All those immigrants seize jobs from American citizens at slave wages.

What happens to the American taxpayer?

"Immigrants are poorer, pay less tax, and are more likely to receive public benefits than American citizens," said Edwin Rubenstein, reporting on the National Research Council's new book: "The New Americans: Economic, Demographics and Fiscal Effects of Immigration." The Social Contract Winter 2007-08.

The NRC found that the average immigrant household receives $13,326 in federal welfare and pays $10,664.00 in federal taxes. Thus, American taxpayers shell out $2,682.00 for each immigrant household. In addition, the report showed that immigrants affect 15 different executive agencies of the U.S. government.

---

[13] <http://www.thesoicalcontract.com/>www.thesoicalcontract.com

Strangling of American Liberty

Earned Income Tax Credit-fraud is rampant and IRS does little to verify existence of children. Clean Air and Climate Change-these goals are unattainable as long as US population grows-driven by unending immigration. Emergency medical treatment-US taxpayer money provides $250 million a year to help hospitals defray costs for illegal aliens. Bureau of Land Management-the Interior Department spends $1 million to mitigate environmental damage done by illegals crossing US southern border. Migrant educational grants-intended to help states educate children of illegal workers. More fraud from over-counting. Office of Foreign Labor Certification-immigrant workers depress wages for US citizens resulting in declines in federal revenues at $100 billion annually.

[14]Katie Couric reported 300,000 pregnant Mexican women cross the border to birth their babies, known as 'anchor babies', in American hospitals at an average cost of $6,000.00 per birth with no complications. If the child suffers heart defects, Downs Syndrome, Autism or any other problems, the costs jump to $500,000.00 with long-term care into the millions of dollars. All footed by the America taxpayer!

 Not mentioned in Couric's report, that child enjoys free breakfasts and lunches through 13 years of publicly funded education at an average cost of $7,000.00 per year. Additionally, American taxpayers foot the bill for all medical and housing assistance for the child and mother. More hidden costs add up with ESL classes to teach the child English. Connecticut alone suffers 120 languages in their schools while Colorado suffers over 40 foreign languages that cripple their classrooms. The list of expenses paid for by American taxpayer soars with time and numbers of illegal aliens. Additionally, legal immigrants sponsor their relatives in chain migration and family reunification at US taxpayer expense. These immigrants take American jobs

---

[14] http://rense.com/general81/dtli.htm

while they burn American taxpayer funds for immigrant welfare. This all happens while the US national debt approaches $20 trillion. Immigrants flood into this country while jobs cascade out to China where we owe $1 trillion in T-bills as of 2008. Additionally, we suffer a $700 billion annual trade deficit.

Once those illegal aliens hit this country, half of them work off the books and do not pay $401 billion dollars annually according to the 2005 Bear Stearns Report. Additionally, they form the second largest underground economy in the world. Both legal and illegal immigrants send $80 billion back to their home countries in cash transfers on untaxed money.,

These are not up-to-date statics, so you can imagine what it is today in the year 2015..

The following article I pulled off the internet.

[15]Illegal immigrants constitute about 4 percent of adults in the United States, but they gave birth to about 8 percent of babies in 2008, according to a study published yesterday by the Pew Hispanic Center. The findings, based on 2009 census data, reveal how illegal immigrants differ from the overall American population in age, fertility and marriage. "This is a population of young, working families. That's what drives these birth numbers," said Jeff Passel, co-author of the study and senior demographer at the Pew Hispanic Center, a nonpartisan research group in Washington, D.C.

The median age of illegal-immigrant adults is 35.5, compared with 45.9 for legal immigrants and 46.3 for American natives, the study found. Of illegal-immigrant adults, 45 percent live with a spouse or partner and a child

---

[15] http://californiawatch.org/dailyreport/eight-percent-us-babies-born-illegal-immigrants-3805

Strangling of American Liberty

or children, compared with 34 percent of legal immigrants and 21 percent of U.S.-born adults. About 85 percent of the parents who are illegal immigrants are Latino, Passel said. Foreign-born Latinos also have higher rates of fertility than their U.S.-born counterparts, whites, blacks and Asians. "You have an accumulation of people here, so they're here, they form families and then they have kids," Passel said. Children born in the U.S. are citizens, regardless of their parents' legal status. Nationwide, 7 percent of children under 18 years old, or 5.1 million kids, have at least one parent in the country illegally. Of those children, 79 percent were born here, the study found. The study comes amid heated debate in Washington over whether to change the 14th Amendment, which grants citizenship to anyone born in the country. A nationwide survey in June by the Pew Research Center for the People & the Press, an affiliate of the Pew Hispanic Center, found 56 percent of people oppose such an amendment, while 41 percent support it. A more recent poll by CNN found an even smaller margin, with 51 percent opposed and 49 percent in favor. The controversy began when Sen. Lindsey Graham, R-S.C., told Fox News "people come here to have babies. They come here to drop a child. It's called 'drop and leave.'" Graham has proposed that birthright citizenship no longer apply to children of illegal immigrants. Research by the Center and others does not support Graham's "drop and leave" claim. The Center reports that among illegal immigrants who give birth, more than 80 percent have been in the country for at least a year or more. Douglas Massey, a Princeton University sociologist who has surveyed Mexicans who come the U.S. illegally, told Political Fact "no one ever mentioned having kids in the U.S." as a reason for migrating. Overall, about 59 percent of the country's illegal immigrants come from Mexico, according to the Center.

All of this is strangling American liberty. We have always been a nation of laws; today those laws are not enforced. President Obama, Eric Holder and others who are in power are making up the laws as they go. Never in our history have we as country been so mislead and misinformed.

Where are the great empires of the past? Where is the Assyrian Empire? The Babylonian Empire? The Roman Empire? You can find what is left of them in museums, in ruins and in a few ancient stone buildings frequented only by modern tourists. Great nations rise and fall! Is it possible that the United States could be returned to ashes, like so many great nations that have gone before?

We cannot help but be impressed by the great empires of the past. The Babylonian Empire ruled the Middle East, and the armies of Nebuchadnezzar were unstoppable. The mighty Roman Empire lasted for 500 years, before falling to the Vandals and the Heruli. World War II saw the blitzkrieg expansion of the Third Reich across Europe and North Africa. Hitler's ambitions included conquest of the Soviet Union, but he failed, and Allied armies pummeled mighty Germany into a rubble heap. Can any nation or empire long endure? Can the U.S. last much longer as a superpower? What does the Bible say about the future of kingdoms, empires and nations?

The Union of Soviet Socialist Republics consisted of 15 republics and one-sixth of the world's land surface, or 2.5 times the area of the U.S. This great superpower reveled in its Communist ideology; it fought for the hearts of nations all over the world and lost. On November 9, 1989, the symbol of its subjugation of Eastern Europe, the Berlin Wall came tumbling down.

Now this once-mighty power has shattered into 15 struggling nation-states, with 12 tied together in the Commonwealth of Independent States. Who could have predicted the fall of this great superpower? The Bible is clear that nations rise and fall. In the Bible, we find 25 scriptures that deal with liberty. We will deal with them in a future chapter.

Strangling of American Liberty

Many things are happening in the world, which seem to conclude Christ coming. They are called, "The signs of the times."

The Divine "scheme of things," as Christianity understands it, is at once extremely elastic and extremely rigid. It is elastic in that it includes a large measure of liberty for the creature; it is rigid in that it includes the proviso that however created beings choose to behave, they must accept responsibility for their own actions and endure the consequences.

The result of all of our actions past and present will bring about the results of our future.

Chapter 5

Downgrading our Military
Obama has downgraded our military:

[16]WASHINGTON – Retired Army Maj. Gen. Patrick Brady, recipient of the U.S. military is highest decoration, the Medal of Honor, as well as other top retired officers, say President Obama's agenda is decimating the morale of the U.S. ranks to the point members no longer feel prepared to fight or have the desire to win.

"There is no doubt he (Obama) is intent on emasculating the military and will fire anyone who disagrees with him" over such issues as "homosexuals, women in foxholes, the Obama sequester," Brady told WND.

"They are purging everyone, and if you want to keep your job, just keep your mouth shut," one source told WND.

Not only are military service members being demoralized and the ranks' overall readiness being reduced by the Obama administration's purge of key leaders, colonels – those lined up in rank to replace outgoing generals – are quietly taking their careers in other directions.

Retired Army Lt. Gen. William G. "Jerry" Boykin, who was with Delta Force and later Deputy under Secretary of Defense for Intelligence under President George W. Bush, says it is worrying that four-star generals are being retired at the rate that has occurred under Obama.

"Over the past three years, it is unprecedented for the number of four-star generals to be relieved of duty, and not necessarily relieved for cause," Boykin said.

---

[16] http://www.wnd.com/2013/10/top-generals-obama-is-purging-the-military/

"I believe there is a purging of the military," he said. "The problem is worse than we have ever seen."

Boykin points out that the military adheres to the constitutional requirement of a civilian leadership over the military. As a consequence, officers are not allowed to criticize their civilian leadership, as occurred when Gen. Stanley A. McChrystal was relieved in 2010 of his command of the International Security Assistance Force and commander of U.S. Forces in Afghanistan.

He was relieved due to what has been described as unflattering remarks made about Vice President Joe Biden and other administration officials in a Rolling Stone magazine article. He was recalled to Washington where Obama accepted his resignation as commander in Afghanistan.

Boykin says that because of the fundamental civilian leadership over the military, McCrystal was "appropriately forced to retire."

Read the words of the Founders, in "America's God and Country Encyclopedia of Quotations."

Some officers were involved in adulterous affairs and those situations, Boykin said, also were grounds for dismissal.

Boykin specifically said that because of the civilian-military relationship, he did not see any prospect for a "coup" coming from the military ranks.

Boykin said that no one in the military has ever raised the issue of a "coup." However, civilians with no military experience have raised this issue with him and commented that the military needs to "fulfill [its] constitutional duty and take over the government,'" Boykin said. He added that he has never raised this issue but only has responded to anyone who has raised these questions by saying that,

"Our Constitution puts a civilian in charge of the military and as a result a coup would not be constitutional. You're not going to see a coup in the military."

Nevertheless, Boykin said the future of the military is becoming more and more of concern, since colonels who would be generals is being relieved of duty, if they show that they are not going to support Obama's agenda, which critics have described as socialist.

"I talk to a lot of folks who don't support where Obama is taking the military, but in the military they can't say anything," Boykin said.

Consequently, he said, the lower grades therefore have decided to leave, having been given the signal that there is no future in the military for them.

Boykin referred to recent reports that Obama has purged some 197 officers in the past five years.

These reports suggest these officers were suspected of disloyalty or disagreed with the Obama administration on policy or force-structure issues. As Boykin pointed out, a number of them have been relieved of duty for no given reason.

"Morale is at an unprecedented low," Boykin said, part of which is due to sequestration.

Sequestration has seriously cut back operational readiness for the military to the point where Boykin said that often they have no ammunition and are unable to conduct training because of the planned cuts.

"These officers want to train for war but are not be allowed to" because of the preoccupation not only with sequestration, but what Boykin said were other concerns surfacing in the military under Obama as commander-in-chief.

He referred specifically to the recent repeal of "Don't Ask, Don't Tell," which now allows openly homosexual personnel in the military. In addition, he said the integration of women into the infantry "will reduce readiness of units." He also was critical of the rules of engagement which he says favor "political correctness over our ability to fight to win."

"The last time we won an all-out war was in 1944," Boykin said. "Now, we don't have the will to win."

Brady, who was a legendary "Dust Off" air ambulance pilot in Vietnam and detailed his experiences in his book, **"Dead Men Flying: Victory in Viet Nam,"** said, "The problem is military people will seldom, while on duty, go on the record over such issues, and many will not ever, no matter how true. "I hear from many off the record who are upset with the current military leadership and some are leaving and have left in the past," he said. Brady referred to additional problems in today's military including "girly-men leadership [and] medals for not shooting and operating a computer. This president will never fight if there is any reason to avoid it and with a helpless military he can just point to our weakness and shrug his shoulders." Brady made similar references in a recent **article** he wrote for WND in which he said, "Just when you thought the leadership of this government could not get any worse, it does. Never in history has an administration spawned another scandal to cover the current one." The reference was to the recent firing of a number of generals to mask "Obama's serial scandals, all prefaced by lies – Fast and Furious, Benghazi, NSA, IRS" among others.

WND reported that three of the nine firings by Obama this year alone were linked to the controversy surrounding the

Sep. 11, 2012, terrorist attack on the CIA special mission in Benghazi, Libya. In one case, U.S. Army Gen. Carter Ham, who commanded U.S. African Command when the consulate was attacked and four Americans were killed, was highly critical of the decision by the State Department not to send in reinforcements. Obama has insisted there were no reinforcements available that night. However, Ham contends reinforcements could have been sent in time, and he said he never was given a stand-down order. However, others contend that he was given the order but defied it. He ultimately was relieved of his command and retired.

Now, new information in the Washington Times reveals there were Delta Force personnel in Tripoli at the time of the attack and two members volunteered to dispatch to Benghazi to assist in protecting the Benghazi compound, contrary to stand-down orders from the State Department. Another flag officer involved in the Benghazi matter – which remains under congressional investigation – was Rear Adm. Charles Gaouette. He commanded the Carrier Strike Group. He contends aircraft could have dispatched to Libya in time to help the Americans under fire. He was later removed from his post for alleged profanity and making "racially insensitive comments." Army Major Gen. Ralph Baker was the commander of the Combined Joint Task Force Horn of Africa at Camp Lemonier in Djibouti, Africa. Baker contended that attack helicopters could have reached the consulate in time on the night of the attack.

Between John Kerry, Barack Obama, and Hillary Clinton you have three of greatest liars in history. The quest for power is all they want.. They could care less about this country and you.

Chapter 6

Religious Liberty

The more we dig the more we can find how we as a country are losing our liberty.

[17]Freedom and discipline have come to be regarded as mutually exclusive, when in fact freedom is not at all the opposite, but the final reward, of discipline. It is to be bought with a high price, not merely claimed... The [professional] skater and [race] horse are free to perform as they do only because they have been subjected to countless hours of grueling work, rigidly prescribed, and faithfully carried out. Men are free to soar into space because they have willingly confined themselves in a tiny capsule designed and produced by highly trained scientists and craftsmen, have meticulously followed instructions and submitted themselves to rules which others defined.

[18]Roger Williams, who fled Massachusetts and founded Rhode Island colony in pursuit of religious liberty, writes in *The Bloody Tenant of Persecution* (1644):

"It is the will and command of God that, since the coming of his Son, the Lord Jesus, a permission of the

---

[17] Elisabeth Elliot in All That Was Ever Ours. Christianity Today, Vol. 32, no. 16.

[18] —"The Baptists: A People Who Gathered 'to Walk in All His Ways,' " Christian History, no. 6.

---

most Paganish, Jewish, Turkish, or antichristian consciences and worships be granted to all men in all nations and countries: and they are only to be fought against with that sword which is only, in soul matters, able to conquer: to wit, the sword of God's Spirit, the Word of God. "God requires not a uniformity of religion to be enacted and enforced in any civil state; which enforced uniformity, sooner or later, is the greatest occasion of civil war, ravishing of conscience, persecution of Christ Jesus in his servants, and of the hypocrisy and destruction of millions of souls. The permission of other consciences and worships than a state professed only can, according to God, procure a firm and lasting peace..." Christians are under attack everywhere. If you take the name of Christ, you can be stabbed, shot, beheaded or burnt alive. This is happing now in countries. The "coming persecution of Christians" has already begun. It is already here. So why is the mainstream media in the United States almost very silent about this phenomenon? When some politician somewhere around the globe inadvertently offends homosexuals or Muslims, it instantly makes headline news. However, very few Americans are even aware that it has been estimated that 100 million Christians are currently facing persecution and that approximately 100,000 Christians die for their faith each year. As you are about to see, Christians all over the world are being burned alive, beheaded, crucified, tortured to death and imprisoned in metal shipping containers just because of what they believe. This persecution goes on:

> [19]Christian Taxi Driver Pulled Out Of His Cab And Beheaded In Egypt: One attack involved taxi driver Rafaat Aziz Mina, who was slaughtered in an Alexandria street just because he was Christian. In his early twenties, he was killed on 16 August by a mob of Islamists who took to the streets after news reached them about the military's action against

---

[19] Pulled from the internet different places

their camps in Cairo. An amateur video shot by a resident shows a mob blocking cars, checking the passengers inside. When Aziz's taxi was stopped, one of the protesters noted a cross hanging from the rear view mirror. Quickly, the young man was dragged out and kicked, punched and beaten to death. For several minutes, the extremists defiled the lifeless body kicking and spitting on it, concluding their performance by cutting off his head, which they left on the sidewalk.

> Tortured To Death By U.S.-Backed Al-Qaeda Rebels in Syria: In late October, the U.S-supported "opposition" invaded and occupied Sadad for over a week, until ousted by the nation's military. Among other atrocities, 45 Christians—including women and children—were killed, several tortured to death; Sadad's 14 churches, some ancient, were ransacked and destroyed; the bodies of six people from one family, ranging from ages 16 to 90, were found at the bottom of a well (an increasingly common fate for "subhuman" Christians).

> "Slaughtering Us like Chickens" In the Central African Republic: Thousands of Christian civilians sought refuge at an airport guarded by French soldiers Friday, fleeing from the mostly Muslim ex-rebels with machetes and guns who rule the country a day after the worst violence to hit the chaotic capital in nine months. When several French helicopters landed at the airport, people sang with joy as they banged on plastic buckets and waved rags into the air in celebration. Outside the barbed wire fences of the airport, bodies lay decomposing along the roads in a capital too dangerous for many to collect the corpses. Thursday's clashes left at least 280 dead, according to national radio, and have raised fears that waves of retaliatory attacks could soon follow. "They are slaughtering us like chickens," said Appolinaire Donoboy, a Christian whose family remained in hiding.

- ➤ Shot For Refusing To Convert To Islam In Libya: A group of Muslims robbed two Egyptian Christians living in Libya, then tied up and shot them to death after the two Copts refused their demand to convert to Islam, relatives said. On a rural road in Derna District in northeastern Libya on Wednesday (Sept. 25), a group of Muslims surrounded Waleed Saad Shaker, and Nash'at Shenouda Ishaq, demanded their belongings and started beating them. During the strong-arm robbery, the relatives said, the Muslims demanded that Shaker and Ishaq recite the shahada, the declaration of conversion to Islam. When the two Orthodox Coptic Christians refused, the group of Muslims tied them up and shot them.

- ➤ Head Cut Off In Front Of A Camera For Converting To Christianity In Tunisia: A young man appears held down by masked men. His head is pulled back, with a knife to his throat. He does not struggle and appears resigned to his fate. Speaking in Arabic, the background speaker, or "narrator," chants a number of Muslim prayers and supplications, mostly condemning Christianity, which, because of the Trinity, is referred to as a polytheistic faith: "Let Allah be avenged on the polytheist apostate"; "Allah empower your religion, make it victorious against the polytheists"; "Allah, defeat the infidels at the hands of the Muslims," and "There is no god but Allah and Muhammad is his messenger."
Then, to cries of "Allahu Akbar!"— Allah is greater!"—the masked man holding the knife to the apostate's throat begins to slice away, severing the head completely after approximately one minute of graphic knife carving, as the victim drowns in blood. Finally, the severed head is held aloft to more Islamic slogans of victory.

- ➤ Fifty Christians Burned to Death in Their Pastor's Home in Nigeria: Fifty members of a northern Nigerian church were burned to death in their pastor's house.

Strangling of American Liberty

The attack by armed gunmen was only the first in a 12-village spree of violence that left over 100 dead in northern Nigeria's Plateau State, a region that had previously been outside Islamic terrorist group Boko Haram's operational area and is the largely Muslim Fulani tribesmen's homeland.

Yet Boko Haram claimed responsibility for the attacks and threatened even more violence.

➢ Two Brothers Crucified For Their Faith In Ivory Coast: Two peasant brothers were brutally crucified on "the example of Christ" as forces loyal to Ivory Coast President Alassane Ouattara continue to target perceived supporters of his ousted Christian predecessor, Laurent Gbagbo.

Raphael Aka Kouame died of his injuries; incredibly, his younger brother, Kouassi Privat Kacou, survived the ordeal. The pair were badly beaten and tortured before being crudely nailed to cross-shaped planks by their hands and feet with steel spikes on 29 May.

➢ Angry Mob Of About 1,000 People Destroys A Church And Beats Christians In India: Shouting religious slogans, a mob estimated at 1,000 people has destroyed a Christian church under construction in northern India, according to a report received from church leaders in the region. The attack occurred Sunday.

With the building demolished, the mob began to beat the pastor, his mother and church members, who were able to flee and went into hiding for the night. The extent of their injuries is not known.

➢ Suicide Bombers Kill 81 at a Church in Pakistan: A pair of suicide bombers killed 81 people outside a church in northwestern Pakistan on Sunday in the deadliest attack yet on the country's Christian minority, reviving fears that the newly installed government is powerless to stop the resurgent Taliban's reign of terror.

➢ The attack on the 19th-century All Saints Church in Peshawar took place as hundreds of worshippers were streaming out of the church, police chief Mohammad Ali Babakhel told the newspaper Dawn.

- ➢ "The suicide bomber tried to attack the people, but when he was stopped by the police, he detonated the bomb," he said. "The second blast was carried out inside the church."

- ➢ 80 Lashes for Drinking Communion Wine in Iran: An Iranian court sentenced four Iranian men to 80 whiplashes for drinking wine during communion and possession of a satellite antenna.
The court issued the sentence in the city of Rasht on October 6. Christian Solidarity Worldwide, an advocacy organization for religious freedom, reported on the punishment last week on its website.

- ➢ Imprisoned In Metal Shipping Containers In Eritrea: A representative of Open Doors, a charity that works with Christians under pressure for their faith, said that many Christian men and women are being held in underground dungeons, metal shipping containers and military detention centers.
"They face exposure, hard labor and insufficient food, water and hygiene. They are regularly denied medical treatment for malaria and pneumonia contracted while in prison or diseases like diabetes, hypertension or cancer that they may have arrived with," said the representative.

- ➢ Publicly Executed For Owning A Bible In North Korea: Eight people — their heads covered with white bags — were tied to stakes at a local stadium in the city of Wonsan, before authorities shot them with a machine gun, according to the source. Wonsan authorities gathered a crowd of 10,000 people, including children, at Shinpoong Stadium and forced them to watch the killings.

For the moment, things like this are not happening in the United States. However, you would have to be extremely naive to think that it never could happen here.

Strangling of American Liberty

Animosity toward Christians is rapidly rising in this country. Anyone that spends much time cruising around the Internet can see that very clearly. In fact, some bloggers recently suggested the castration and murder of Christians here in the United States.

Look at the beheadings.
It might seem easy to dismiss those remarks as the ramblings of a few deranged individuals, but the truth is that our own government is now labeling Christians as "extremists" and "potential terrorists All over the planet, the persecution of Christians is growing. In addition, our own government is now demonizing us and characterizing us as a "threat". However, the governments of the western world and the mainstream media are almost entirely ignoring what is happening. People need to know the reality of the holocaust that is happening. Sadly, the vast majority of Americans have never even heard about any of the stories I have shared.

Chapter 7

Redistribution of Wealth

As we look at this subject, we need to see it is one of the tenants of the faith of Islam. One must remember President Obama grew up in Islamic culture. Attending a school in Jakarta, Indonesia, he was registered as a Muslim. He was also a member of "Trinity United Church of Christ". The church is located in Chicago. To understand Obama and his approach you must look at the Black Value system of the church he attended for twenty years. Below you will find what they believe. **I copied this off the Trinity Web site. I have underlined important statements.**

[20]**The Black Value System**

Trinity United Church of Christ adopted the Black Value System, written by the Manford Byrd Recognition Committee, chaired by the late Vallmer Jordan in 1981. Dr. Manford Byrd, our brother in Christ, withstood the ravage of being denied his earned ascension to the number one position in the Chicago School System. His dedication to the pursuit of excellence, despite systematic denials, has inspired the congregation of Trinity United Church of Christ. Prayerfully, we have called upon the wisdom of all past generations of suffering Blacks for guidance in fashioning an instrument of Black self-determination, the Black Value System.

Beginning in 1982, an annual Black Value System – Educational Scholarship in the name of Dr. Byrd was instituted. The first recipient of the Dr. Manford Byrd Award, which is given annually to the man or woman who best exemplifies the Black Value System, was our brother, Dr. Manford Byrd.

---

[20] The Black Value system Trinity Church of Christ

Strangling of American Liberty

These Black Ethics must be taught and exemplified in homes, churches, nurseries and schools, wherever Blacks are gathered. They consist of the following concepts: Commitment to God. "The God of our weary years" will give us the strength to give up prayerful passivism and become Black Christian Activists, soldiers for Black freedom and the dignity of all humankind. Matthew 22:37 – Thou shalt love the Lord thy God with all thy heart, and with all thy soul, and with all thy mind.

Commitment to the Black Community. The highest level of achievement for any Black person must be a contribution of strength and continuity of the Black Community. I John 4:20 – If a man say, I love God, and hateth his brother [or his sister], he is a liar; for he that loveth not his brother or sister whom he hath seen, how can he love God whom he hath not seen?

Commitment to the Black Family. The Black family circle must generate strength, stability and love, despite the uncertainty of externals, because these characteristics are required if the developing person is to withstand warping by our racist competitive society. Those Blacks who are blessed with membership in a strong family unit must reach out and expand that blessing to the less fortunate. Deuteronomy 6:6-8 – And these words, which I command thee this day, shall be in thine heart: And thou shalt teach them diligently unto thy children, and shalt talk of them when thou sittest in thine house, and when thou walkest by the way, and when thou liest down, and when thou risest up. In addition, thou shalt bind them for a sign upon thine hand, and they shall be as frontlets between thine eyes. **Dedication to the Pursuit of Education**. We must forswear anti-intellectualism. Continued survival demands that each Black person be developed to the utmost of his/her mental potential despite the inadequacies of the formal education process. "Real education" fosters understanding of us as well as every aspect of our environment. In addition, it develops within us the ability to fashion concepts and tools for better utilization of our resources, and more effective solutions to our problems. Since the majority of Blacks have been denied such learning, Black Education must include elements that produce high school graduates with marketable skills, a trade or qualifications for apprenticeships, or proper preparation for college. Basic education for all Blacks should include Mathematics, Science, Logic, General Semantics, Participative Politics, Economics and Finance, and the Care and Nurture of Black minds. Matthew 22:37 – Thou shalt love the Lord thy God with all thy heart, and with all thy soul and with all thy mind.

Dedication to the Pursuit of Excellence. To the extent that we individually reach for, even strain for excellence, we increase, geometrically, the value and resourcefulness of the Black Community. We must recognize the relativity of one's best; this year's best can be bettered next year. Such is the language of growth and development. We must seek to excel in every endeavor. Ecclesiastes 9:10 – Whatsoever thy hand findeth to do, do [it] with thy might; for [there is] no work, nor device, nor knowledge, nor wisdom, in the grave, whither thou goest.

Adherence to the Black Work Ethic. "It is becoming harder to find qualified people to work in Chicago." Whether this is true or not, it represents one of the many reasons given by businesses and industries for deserting the Chicago area. We must realize that a location with good facilities, adequate transportation and a reputation for producing skilled workers will attract industry. We are in competition with other cities, states and nations for jobs. High productivity must be a goal of the Black workforce. II Thessalonians 3:7-12 – For yourselves know how ye ought to follow us: for we behaved not ourselves disorderly among you; Neither did we eat any man's bread for nought; but wrought with labor and travail night and day, that we might not be chargeable to any of you: Not because we have not power, but to make ourselves an ensample unto you to follow us. For even when we were with you, this we commanded you, that if any would not work, neither should he eat. For we hear that there are some which walk among you disorderly, working not at all, but are busybodies. Now them that are such we command and exhort by our Lord Jesus Christ, that with quietness they work, and eat their own bread.

Commitment to Self-Discipline and Self-Respect. To accomplish anything worthwhile requires self-discipline. We must be a community of self-disciplined persons if we are to actualize and utilize our own human resources, instead of perpetually submitting to exploitation by others. Self-discipline, coupled with a respect for self, will enable each of us to be an instrument of Black Progress and a model for Black Youth. I Peter 1:4-7 – To an inheritance incorruptible, and undefiled, and that fadeth not away, reserved in heaven for you, Who are kept by the power of God through faith unto salvation ready to be revealed in the last time. Wherein ye greatly rejoice, though now for a season, if need be, ye are in heaviness through manifold temptations: That the trial of your faith, being much more precious than of gold that perishes, though it be tried with fire, might be found unto praise and honor and glory at the appearing of Jesus Christ.

Disavowal of the Pursuit of "Middleclassness." Classic methodology on control of captives teaches that captors must be able to identify the "talented tenth" of those subjugated, especially those who show promise of providing the kind of leadership that might threaten the captor's control. Proverbs 3:13-14 – Happy are those who find wisdom and those who gain understanding, for her income is better than silver and her revenue better than gold. Those so identified are separated from the rest of the people by: Killing them off directly, and/or fostering a social system that encourages them to kill off one another. Placing them in concentration camps, and/or structuring an economic environment that induces captive youth to fill the jails and prisons.

Seducing them into a socioeconomic class system, which, while training them to earn more dollars, hypnotizes them into believing they are better than others are and teaches them to think in terms of "we" and "we"" instead of "us." Therefore, while it is permissible to chase "middleclassness" with all our might, we must avoid the third separation method – the psychological entrapment of Black "middleclassness." If we avoid this snare, we will also diminish our "voluntary" contributions to methods A and B. In addition, more importantly, Black people no longer will be deprived of their birthright: the leadership, resourcefulness and example of their own talented persons.

Pledge to Make the Fruits of All Developing and Acquired Skills Available to the Black Community.
Pledge to Allocate Regularly, a Portion of Personal Resources for Strengthening and Supporting Black Institutions.

Pledge Allegiance to All Black Leadership Who Espouse and Embrace the Black Value System.
Personal Commitment to Embracement of the Black Value System. To measure the worth and validity of all activity in terms of positive contributions to the general welfare of the Black Community and the Advancement of Black People towards freedom.
After reading the above statement, you can see it is racist to the core. Now, I would like to show you the doctrine of the Nation of Islam, which is affiliated with this church. Many African-Americans, including some Christians, regard the Nation of Islam as a Christian organization that is a positive motivating factor in the black community. A review of their basic beliefs, however, will demonstrate that the Nation of Islam is one of the fastest-growing American cults.
The whole basis of the beliefs or theology of the Nation of Islam is an attempt to answer two major questions: (1) "Who are we as a people?" and (2) "What is sin?" **The Nation of Islam denies the essentials of the historic Christian faith. The following list of beliefs includes excerpts from the Nation of Islam's own writings.**
Polytheism. The Nation of Islam is a polytheistic religion. Several references in their literature point to a belief in many gods, and there is reference to a council of 24 scientist-gods who write history. One of them acts as God,

Strangling of American Liberty

while the others do the work of getting the future together for the Nation. Black men are themselves referred to as being gods. "You [the black man] are walking around looking for a God to bow to and worship. You are the God!" The Gods Are Not Eternal. According to the Nation of Islam, although the spirit of Allah (God) lives on, the gods are not eternal. "We all know that there was a God in the beginning that created all these things and do know that He does not exist today."

God Is a Man. They teach that Allah "came to us from the Holy City of Mecca, Arabia, in 1930. He used the name of Wallace D. Fard. God is a man and we just cannot make Him other than man, lest we make Him an inferior one; for man's intelligence has no equal in other than man."

"Yakub Myth." A basic teaching in their belief system is the "Yakub myth." Yakub was one of the council of 24 black scientist-gods. He rebelled against Allah and the council, causing havoc. He created the white race as a race of devils to strike back at the black race. Elijah Muhammad said that black people are not sinners, but that the white man is at fault for their problems.

The Trinity. The Nation of Islam denies the Trinity. "The Christians refer to God as a 'Mystery' and a 'Spirit' and divide Him into thirds. One part they call the Father, another part the Son, and the third part they call the Holy Ghost — which makes the three, one. This is contrary to both nature and mathematics. The law of mathematics will not allow us to put three into one." "Making the Son and the Holy Ghost the equal with the Father is absolutely sinful."

Deity of Christ. The Nation of Islam rejects the essential Christian doctrine that Jesus is both God and man. Jesus "did not consider himself to be God or a son of God or equal of Him...Jesus was only a man and prophet of Allah." In a four-hour videotape of Louis Farrakhan's 1994 Easter Service, "The Crucifixion of Jesus: The Imprisonment of Minister Farrakhan," Farrakhan discusses the crucifixion and relates it to himself, saying, "I am hanging on the cross right now. I am on Calvary right now and the more I suffer, the more our people are raised to consciousness...you do not have to look for Jesus. I represent him. I was born to die for you and I love the thought of dying for you."

The Holy Spirit. The Nation of Islam denies that the Holy Spirit is God. They view the Spirit as a "spook."
The so-called Negroes think of God in terms of something without form (spirit or spook) and they believe that His throne is somewhere in the sky....The teachings of Christianity have put God out of Man into nothing (spirit). Can you imagine God without form but yet interested in our affairs who are the human beings? What glory would an immaterial God get out of a material world? We also learn that a spirit is not self-independent; it is dependent upon air, water and food. Without it, the spirit can have no life. So how can a spirit be God?

The Bible. Although they do make use of it when it does not contradict their own teachings, the Nation of Islam believes the Bible has been tampered with by the white man. "The Bible is now being called the Poison Book by God Himself, and who can deny that it is not poison?...the Book can't be recognized as the pure and Holy Word of God."

Atonement and Salvation. The Nation of Islam rejects the essential Christian doctrines of atonement and salvation. "We know we have a Savior. In 1877 a Savior was born [i.e., Wallace Fard]....A Savior is born, not to save the Jews but to save the poor Negro....A Savior has come to save you from sin, not because you are by nature a sinner but because you have followed a sinner."

The Human Race. As we have seen, the Nation of Islam teaches a racist doctrine that the black race is divine and righteous by nature. They were the creators of the universe, and they are taught they are black gods.
Heaven and Hell. Members of the Nation of Islam do not believe in the hereafter, whether it is heaven or hell. "I have no alternative than to tell you that there is not any life

beyond the grave. There is no justice in the sweet bye and bye. Immortality is NOW, HERE." To the Nation of Islam, heaven and hell are regarded as special conditions here on earth now, not as special places to go after death. "The Christians say, 'Confess the Lord Jesus Christ or you (who are other than the Christians) will burn in hell forever.' That hell must not be so hot that one can burn in it forever and never burn up."

The Nation of Islam teaches other anti-Christian doctrines besides those that have been cited above. However, the examples we have considered are certainly among the most significant and should be sufficient to acquaint you with their theology.

It is very clear "The Nation of Islam" is associated with the church in Chicago. The following was taken off the internet. [21]Trinity is well within the mainstream of the black church, and is remarkable in the mainline world only for its size and influence and for its handful of celebrity members, like Oprah Winfrey and hip-hop artist Common.

As noted on Biography.com Farrakhan, Louis (1933-): "Black Muslim leader. Born Louis Eugene Walcott on May 11, 1933 in the Bronx, New York. He grew up in Roxbury, Massachusetts, and was converted to the Nation of Islam by Malcolm X. Following Malcolm X's defection (1963-4), Farrakhan became the national representative for Elijah Muhammad...In 1995, along with other prominent black leaders such as Al Sharpton and Barack Obama, Farrakhan helped lead the Million Man March on Washington.

It should be also be noted that as reported in the New York Post of January 18, BARACK'S UN-RIGHTEOUS REV: "In a 2007 interview with The New York Times, Wright said: "When [Obama's] enemies find out that in 1984 I went to Tripoli [to visit Moammar Khadafy] with Farrakhan, a lot of his Jewish support will dry up quicker than a snowball in hell.""

---

[21] groups.google.com/

Obama's campaign released a statement from the senator on January 15.

"I decry racism and anti-Semitism in every form and strongly condemn the anti-Semitic statements made by Minister Farrakhan," Obama said in the statement. "I assume that Trumpet Magazine made its own decision to honor Farrakhan based on his efforts to rehabilitate ex-offenders, but it is not a decision with which I agree."

The statement ignored the point that his minister and friend had spoken adoringly of Farrakhan and that Wright's church was behind the "Rev. Dr. Jeremiah A. Wright Jr. Lifetime Achievement Trumpeteer award" on Farrakhan to the Nation of Islam leader. Award was presented at the 2007 Trumpet Gala held on November 2, at the Hyatt Regency Chicago. Not only is Trumpet owned and produced by Wright's church out of the church's offices, Wright's daughters serve as publisher and executive editor of the magazine.

"When Minister Louis Farrakhan speaks, America listens...For his commitment to truth, education and leadership, we honor Minister Louis Farrakhan with the Rev. Jeremiah W. Wright Jr. Lifetime Achievement Award."

Cohen reported in the Post that Obama's chief strategist, David Axelrod, had said that Obama and his minister disagree on many issues and Farrakhan was one of them. Prior to Obama's statement of January 15, (The Award was presented November 9, two months prior to his statement.) he did not denounce ties between Pastor Wright and Farrakhan, nor has Obama rejected the anti-Israel diatribes of Wright. Nor did Obama denounce Farrakhan when he helped lead the Million Man March in 1995 in Washington. One has to ask if in his condemnation of the remarks of Farrakhan, he is also condemning the Nation of Islam.

Obama's confusion and misunderstandings of religion and White & Black relations has led him in his decisions. Actually, Obama cannot make a decision and

Strangling of American Liberty

because of that, American liberty is being strangled. Most people are too busy to do the research and accept what others might say. Now I would like to show you how Islam is playing a big part in Obama's structure of our present government.

The financial obligation upon Muslims

An important principle of Islam is that everything belongs to God, and that wealth is therefore held by human beings in trust. The word zakah means both "purification" and "growth." As quoted by Islamic doctrine, "Our possessions are purified by setting aside a proportion for those in need and for the society in general. Like the pruning of plants, this cutting back balances and encourages new growth. Each Muslim calculates his or her own *zakah* individually. This involves the annual payment of a fortieth of one's capital, excluding such items as primary residence, car and professional tools.

An individual may also give as much as he or she pleases as sadaqa-h, and does so preferably in secret. Although this word can be translated as "voluntary charity", it has a wider meaning.

The Prophet said, "Even meeting your brother with a cheerful face is an act of charity." The Prophet also said: "Charity is a necessity for every Muslim." He was asked: "What if a person has nothing?" The Prophet replied: "He should work with his own hands for his benefit and then give something out of such earnings in charity." The Companions of the Prophet asked: "What if he is not able to work?" The Prophet said: "He should help the poor and needy." The Companions further asked: "What if he cannot do even that?" The Prophet said: "He should urge others to do good." The Companions said: "What if he lacks that also?" The Prophet said: "He should check himself from doing evil. That is also an act of charity."

When looking at this statement we find it is the doctrine of distribution of wealth.

The support of this doctrine is found in the Quran.

[9.60] Alms are only for the poor and the needy, and the officials (appointed) over them, and those whose hearts are made to incline (to truth) and the (ransoming of) captives and those in debts and in the way of Allah and the wayfarer; an ordinance from Allah; and Allah is knowing, Wise.

[2.43] And keep up prayer and pay the poor-rate and bow down with those who bow down.

[2.110] And keep up prayer and pay the poor-rate and whatever good you send before for yourselves, you shall find it with Allah; surely Allah sees what you do. [2.277] Surely they who believe and do good deeds and keep up prayer and pay the poor-rate they shall have their reward from their Lord, and they shall have no fear, nor shall they grieve.

Redistribution of wealth develops a two-class system, wealthy and poor. In our travels around the world, we have found most countries have two classes. People are extremely wealthy or very poor. More than 80 percent of the world's population lives in countries where income differentials are widening. The poorest 40 percent of the world's population accounts for 5 percent of global income. The richest 20 percent accounts for three-quarters of world income. According to UNICEF, 22,000 children die each day due to poverty. In addition, they "die quietly in some of the poorest villages on earth, far removed from the scrutiny and the conscience of the world. Being meek and weak in life makes these dying multitudes even more invisible in death." Around 27-28 percent of all children in developing countries are estimated to be underweight or stunted. The two regions that account for the bulk of the deficit are South Asia and sub-Saharan Africa. If current trends continue, the Millennium Development Goals target of halving the proportion of underweight children will be missed by 30 million children, largely because of slow progress in Southern Asia and sub-Saharan Africa.

What is Capitalism?

Also called free enterprise, private enterprise. an economic systembased on the private ownership of the means of production,distribution, and exchange, characterized by the freedom of capitaliststo operate or manage their properor profit in competitive conditions.

What is Socialism?

Theory or system of social organization that advocates the vesting of the ownership and control of the means of production and distribution, of capital, land, etc., in the community as a whole. Procedure or practice in accordance with this theory. In Marxist theory) the stage following capitalism in the transition of a society to communism, characterized by the imperfect implementation of collectivist principles.

Chapter 8

Biblical; Liberty

[22]Freedom does not mean the absence of constraints or moral absolutes. Suppose a skydiver at 10,000 feet announces to the rest of the group, "I'm not using a parachute this time. I want freedom!"

The fact is that a skydiver is constrained by a greater law—the law of gravity. But when the skydiver chooses the "constraint" of the parachute, she is free to enjoy the exhilaration.

God's moral laws act the same way: they restrain, but they are necessary to enjoy the exhilaration of real freedom.

The Year of Jubilee

Leviticus 25:10 And ye shall hallow the fiftieth year, and **proclaim liberty** throughout *all* the land unto all the inhabitants thereof:
This was very important for it shall be a jubilee unto you; and ye shall return every man unto his possession, and ye shall return every man unto his family. There was the law governing the Year of Jubilee. The Sabbatical Year of rest was not all that God set aside for His people. He also established the Year of Jubilee. Jubilee refers to a fifty-year celebration of liberty, freedom, and redemption. The Year of Jubilee proclaimed one of the greatest messages God ever gave His people: the message of freedom and redemption. It is the message inscribed on the Liberty Bell of the United States of America: "Proclaim liberty throughout all the land" In the Year of Jubilee everyone

---

[22] Today's Best Illustrations - Today's Best Illustrations – Volumes 1-4.

and everything was set free. If a person had sold or mortgaged his land, it was set free and returned to the original owner. If a person had sold himself or his labor as a slave in order to eat and live, he was set free. All debts and financial obligations were written off as well as all labor obligations. All obligations and enslavements due to debt were wiped out. All land was returned to the family of the original owner and every owner and family member returned to his family homestead. As we continue to go in the direction our leadership is leading us, we are moving farther away from liberty. Government regulation is strangling our liberty. In the Year of Jubilee every debt was paid: every person was set free to return home. So it is with the day of salvation. Jesus Christ paid the debt of sin for the believer: the note of debt against the believer is canceled by Christ and the believer is set free by Christ. He canceled the note of debt. Jesus Christ sets the true believer free.

Free at last

Psalms 119:45 And I will **walk at liberty**: for I seek thy precepts.

[23]Luther renders it, "freely." The Septuagint, "in a broad place." The Hebrew word means "wide, broad, large, and spacious." The reference is to that which is free and open; that in which there are no limits, checks, restraints; where a man does what he pleases. The meaning here is, that he would feel he was free. He would not be restrained by evil passions and corrupt desires. He would be delivered from those things which seemed to fetter his goings. This does not here refer so much to external troubles or hindrances, to being oppressed and straitened by external foes, as to internal enemies—to the servitude of sin—to the slavery of appetite and passion. For I seek thy precepts I seek or endeavor to obey them. I seek them as the guide of my life. I ask nothing else to direct me.

---

[23] Barnes Notes

The Lord Jesus will proclaim liberty

Isaiah 61:1 The Spirit of the Lord GOD *is* upon me; because the LORD hath anointed me to preach good tidings unto the meek; he hath sent me to bind up the brokenhearted, to **proclaim liberty** to the captives, and the opening of the prison to *them that are* bound;

A Covenant of Liberty

Jeremiah 34:8 *This is* the word that came unto Jeremiah from the LORD, after that the king Zedekiah had made a covenant with all the people which *were* at Jerusalem, to **proclaim liberty** unto them;

Liberty must be proclaimed
Jeremiah 34:15 And ye were now turned, and had done right in my sight, in **proclaiming liberty** every man to his neighbour; and ye had made a covenant before me in the house which is called by my name:

When the Government takes away your liberty
Jeremiah 34:16 But ye turned and polluted my name, and caused every man his servant, and every man his handmaid, whom ye **had set at liberty** at their pleasure, to return, and brought them into subjection, to be unto you for servants and for handmaids.

Liberty is worth fighting for
Jeremiah 34:17 Therefore thus saith the LORD; Ye have not hearkened unto me, in **proclaiming liberty,** every one to his brother, and every man to his neighbour: behold, I proclaim a liberty for you, saith the LORD, to the sword, to the pestilence, and to the famine; and I will make you to be removed into all the kingdoms of the earth.

JUBILEE

Strangling of American Liberty

Ezekiel 46:17 But if he give a gift of his inheritance to one of his servants, then it shall be his to the **year of liberty**; after it shall return to the prince: but his inheritance shall be his sons' for them. To the year of liberty - That is, to the year of jubilee, called the year of liberty, because there was then a general release. All servants had their liberty, and all alienated estates returned to their former owners.

Liberty is set free from the bondage of sin
Luke 4:18 The Spirit of the Lord *is* upon me, because he hath anointed me to preach the gospel to the poor; he hath sent me to heal the brokenhearted, to preach deliverance to the captives, and recovering of sight to the blind, **to set at liberty them that are bruised,**

Liberty is the freedom to witness
Acts 24:23 And he commanded a centurion to keep Paul, and to let *him* have liberty, and that he should forbid none of his acquaintance to minister or come unto him.

Standing up for Christ is the price you pay for Liberty
Acts 26:32 Then said Agrippa unto Festus, This man might have been set at liberty, if he had not appealed unto Caesar.

Liberty brings freedom to your friends
Acts 27:3 And the next *day* we touched at Sidon. And Julius courteously entreated Paul, and gave *him* liberty to go unto his friends to refresh himself.

Once saved you are at liberty
Romans 8:21 Because the creature itself also shall be delivered from the bondage of corruption into the glorious liberty of the children of God.

Freedom to marry when you partner (wife or husband) dies
1 Corinthians 7:39 The wife is bound by the law as long as her husband liveth; but if her husband be dead, she is

at liberty to be married to whom she will; only in the Lord.

Do not take advantage of your liberty
1 Corinthians 8:9 But take heed lest by any **means this liberty of yours become a stumblingblock** to them that are weak.

Taking advantage of another person liberty is wrong
1 Corinthians 10:29 Conscience, I say, not thine own, but of the other: for why is my liberty judged of another *man's* conscience?

Where God is liberty is
2 Corinthians 3:17 Now the Lord is that Spirit: and where the Spirit of the Lord *is*, there *is* liberty.

Others seek you out to infringe on your liberty
Galatians 2:4 And that because of false brethren unawares brought in, who came in privily to spy out our liberty which we have in Christ Jesus, that they might bring us into bondage:

Stand in the liberty God has given to you
Galatians 5:1 Stand fast therefore in the liberty wherewith Christ hath made us free, and be not entangled again with the yoke of bondage.

As a child of God you are called to liberty
Galatians 5:13 For, brethren, ye have been called unto liberty; only *use* not liberty for an occasion to the flesh, but by love serve one another.

Liberty gives you the joy of sharing with others
Hebrews 13:23 Know ye that *our* brother Timothy is set at liberty; with whom, if he come shortly, I will see you.

Liberty maintained take work and guidance
James 1:25 But whoso looketh into the perfect law of liberty, and continueth *therein*, he being not a forgetful hearer, but a doer of the work, this man shall be blessed in

his deed.

We are judged by the law of liberty. How we use it or abuse it.
James 2:12 So speak ye, and so do, as they that shall be judged by the law of liberty.

Don't use liberty to gain your own interest
1 Peter 2:16 As free, and not using *your* liberty for a cloke of maliciousness, but as the servants of God.

Those who take advantage of liberty are servants of corruption
2 Peter 2:19 While they promise them liberty, they themselves are the servants of corruption: for of whom a man is overcome, of the same is he brought in bondage.

Chapter 9

Conclusion

With all that we have looked at, where do we stand?
America is no different from any other nation and
eventually its sins are going to catch up with it.
Looking back at some great nations, we can see one
nation stands out and that is Rome. Speculations about its
fall very yet somethings stand out with all of those who
researched the matter. Some believe the decay of morality
and lack of Christian premise brought about the fall.
Another reason was the migration of people causing
economic chaos and the value of money declined bringing
about a disaster in its financial system.

In The History of the Decline and Fall of the Roman Empire
(1776–88), Edward Gibbon famously placed the blame on
a loss of civic virtue among the Roman citizens. They
gradually entrusted the role of defending the Empire to
barbarian mercenaries who eventually turned on them.
Gibbon held that Christianity contributed to this shift by
making the populace less interested in the worldly here-
and-now because it was willing to wait for the rewards of
heaven.

The decline of Rome was the natural and inevitable effect
of immoderate greatness. Prosperity ripened the principle
of decay; the causes of destruction multiplied with the
extent of conquest; and as soon as time or accident had
removed the artificial supports, the stupendous fabric
yielded to the pressure of its own weight.

Writing in the 5th century, the Roman historian Vegetius
pleaded for reform of what must have been a greatly
weakened army. The historian Arther Ferrill has suggested
that the Roman Empire – particularly the military – declined
largely as a result of an influx of Germanic mercenaries

into the ranks of the legions. This "Germanization" and the resultant cultural dilution or "barbarization" led not only to a decline in the standard of drill and overall military preparedness within the Empire, but also to a decline of loyalty to the Roman government in favor of loyalty to commanders. Ferrill agrees with other Roman historians such as A.H.M. Jones:

...the decay of trade and industry was not a cause of Rome's fall. There was a decline in agriculture and land was withdrawn from cultivation, in some cases on a very large scale, sometimes as a direct result of barbarian invasions. However, the chief cause of the agricultural decline was high taxation on the marginal land, driving it out of cultivation. Jones is surely right in saying that taxation was spurred by the huge military budget and was thus 'indirectly' the result of the barbarian invasion.

When you look at the points above you can see America is falling right into character.

- Christian values failed
- Economic chaos do to the migration of other countries putting financial pressure on the nation
- The military was made up of more foreign people then those who loved the country
- The lack of loyalty of the people for one another and country
- In contrast with the declining empire theories, historians such as Arnold J. Toynbee and James Burke argue that the Roman Empire itself was a rotten system from its inception, and that the entire Imperial era was one of steady decay of institutions founded in Republican times. In their view, the Empire could never have lasted longer than it did without radical reforms that no Emperor could implement. The Romans had no budgetary system and thus wasted whatever resources they had available. The economy of the Empire was a

Raubwirtschaft or plunder economy based on looting existing resources rather than producing anything new. The Empire relied on riches from conquered territories (this source of revenue ending, of course, with the end of Roman territorial expansion) or on a pattern of tax collection that drove small-scale farmers into destitution (and onto a dole that required even more exactions upon those who could not escape taxation), or into dependency upon a landed élite exempt from taxation. With the cessation of tribute from conquered territories, the full cost of their military machine had to be borne by the citizenry.

- Under the Obama ministration, our national debt now exceeds eighteen trillion dollars. He has increased taxes in some cases by twenty percent. He has attacked farms and small business placing one of the largest burdens in our history on them. His push for Obama care has brought our medical system into total chaos with the price of medical care up over twenty percent in some cases.
- His position on our military has brought about moral decay with the homosexuality policy of equality. His foreign policy decisions has brought about a decay in our relationship with those who were in the same corner as we are.
- His rubbing shoulder with Arabic League of nations has advance their cause and now Iran is on the verge of a nuclear weapon.
- The relationship we have with Israel is in trouble and Israel may have to go it on its own against Iran.
- Our false dependency on oil has enriched those who supply foreign oil.
- The regulations that are placed on business and people who want to work has caused our work force to decline. Our unemployment may be 5.5% but if you were to look at our work force and the number of people who are living off of welfare it would exceed 14%.

- The books just do not balance. I believe if the people of this great country could understand our financial arrangement they would find total mismanagement of money as Rome had before it fell.
- We do not have a balanced system, we spend more on welfare and reform then we are bringing in. The 1% of wealthy people are paying all the taxes. Over 47% of the American people are living on one of the social programs in place.
- With the retiring of the baby boomers, the millenniums will have to pay the bill.
- The increase in the minimum wage to $15 hour will not increase the jobs but will cause a loss of jobs.
- The radicals on the liberal side are ruling and with their rule you have total chaos which could lead to anarchy.
- Obama wants a imperialistic government. He wants to be a king and every move and executive order he has signed was for his own agenda.

Five years from now we will either be better off in total free fall..

What can we do to stop this insanity?

If we act now and stop Obama agenda, we might come out of this in the next ten years.

We cannot afford another liar and misfit in the White House and that leaves out Hillary Clinton.

Regulations, Taxes and values must be put back in place. This means the appeal of many executive orders of Obama.

We must take our schools back and put discipline in them.

We must put shop classes back in the High School to train individuals to do the labor jobs.

Immigration has to come under control and that starts with securing the border. The next step is for everyone who is in this country illegally must report into a location and register to a plan to be equal citizen. All of those who do not report in and are found will be deported back to their own country. It should be a privilege to live in America and one should want to earn that privilege.

Everyone should pay taxes, rich and poor and this is why we need a flat tax. When everyone is paying, no one can complain.

Religious liberty needs to be enforced. Our country is not operated by a religion yet it has always had Judo-Christian ethics. No religion should set the premise for our rights. Rights are a privilege and should be earned. This means to be an American Citizen you should be able to communicate in English and should not be given citizenship until you can speak English.

Private communities should not be given the opportunity to govern under their cultural laws but must abide by the American way. No person should be able to run for elected office until they have lived in America for fifteen years and have a record of accomplishment of being a law-abiding citizen.

We are failing because of a lack of discipline.

Our schools are failing, our prisons are failing and families are failing. We need to back in time and remember what worked.

1. We need install a draft for one year.
    Every young man should have to serve in the military for at least one year. The purpose behind this is to instill discipline. The children of today are so unruly and

government regulation has caused that. Gangs and ghetto areas need to be cleaned up.

2. We need to send all of those who go to prison accept killers, hard-core crimes to the military for three years of hard training under full discipline. If they are able to adjust and work in society, they can serve four years and decide if they want serve or go back into society. This is a special camp use to train hard corps un-disciplined people. This would save the country millions of dollars.

3. Our school must have discipline and when parents refuse to discipline and take care of their children they need to be sent to a military boot camp.

4. Woman should have the privilege of serving but not with men until they have served at least two years.

5. No more private rooms but barracks where they can learn to get along,

6. Parents need to stand up and discipline there children and work with schools. The government needs to stay out of the home. The teachers should be able to discipline children who refuse to listen and are rebellious.

7. Parents need to take responsibility for the children God has given them.

What about religions?

In the United States, freedom of religion is a constitutionally protected right provided in the religion clauses of the First Amendment. Freedom of religion is also closely associated with separation of church and state, a concept advocated by Colonial founders such as Roger Williams, William Penn and later founding fathers such as James Madison and Thomas Jefferson. In accordance to our constitution, we have freedom of religion in this country. Balance is the key to many religions. We have the right to worship whom we please but the fathers of this nation did not leave out God. One religious group should not have more authority then another and should be governed by the laws of the majority who adopted them and voted for them. Government infringement should only step in when the religious group avoids the constitution. The moral laws of America are what have kept us free. People who come to America and bring their culture and religion with them need to understand they are in America and must abide by our rules. They can worship whom they want, that does not give them a special privilege to force their belief on American people.

Any religious group who goes beyond the Constitution should be prosecuted to protect the people from the infringement of a theory. The Bible should be the only authority in America. I f what we do in life goes beyond the decency and morality of life as so purposed by the Bible it should not be allowed. If two men want to be together as husband and wife in their home that is their privilege. Yet, they should not have the privilege of pressing their views on society. Our government should never grant them a marriage license or force the clergy to marry them. As a nation for over two hundred years, those who lived in America did not accept a gay life style. It was not until the sixties this life style was pushed. Rights and morality must work hand and hand. When rights usurp the moral law, you have moral chaos. We have always been a country with limitations as to moral law. Rome fell because of the decline of moral law. Germany fell during WWII because of the decline of moral law.

Judgment will come when God decides to judge. History reveals that God steps in when people are so oppressed by others.

Strangling of American Liberty

Party affiliation should not determine law, this is the privilege of the people.

All of the above is a reality and should not be considered an over-extended government. Government is good when its position is maintaining the law not changing the moral structure of the nation. The moral structure of government changes when immigration has allowed too many people of one group into the United States. We as a nation have lost our balance and the governing society has changed our moral society.

I know this is going to sound racist but the facts prove me out. In the 1960's we imposed on the Black, communities equal rights and privilege as stated in the constitution. There was nothing wrong with helping people attain a greater goal in life. When the groups of people have a different culture then those who are ruling you can expect problems. We all are made in the image of God yet many cultures live in squander and have no intention of changing. The question is this, how much has the Black communities changed in the last fifty years. The moral structure of the Black communities has not changed and what it has done is changed the moral values of other races living in America. Our youth today are lazy and do not want to work. We have over forty present of the people on welfare. Over 80% of Black children are born out wedlock. The White community is catching up with over fifty present of children born out of wedlock. The home has deteriorated and the family structure is gone. I disagreed with the way Blacks were treated when I was growing up yet at the same time, my parents warned me to not marry a Black girl. To some that is prejudice, no it is Biblical. God continued to warn the nation Israel about marrying outside of its culture. The influence that Ishmael had on Isaac was seen by

Sarah and this why she told Abraham to get rid of him. Gen 21.. The group you run with influences you. When you mix several cultures, one is going to dominate. Most of the time it is the lesser of values who wins out. Where you have no discipline, you can expect people to follow that society rather than a structured society. Free love started in the sixties and with it came a unruly group of people. This unruly society came about because of the lack of parental guidance. The burning of draft cards, free love, demonstrations in the streets all of this was the starting of the deterioration of America. The church once was the house of prayer and sacred, today in many places it is a big jam session. The church value system has deteriorated. Anything goes, homosexual marriages, marriage between the races and very few limitations. Those who believe that this is wrong are called bigots. Unruly people if given enough time will destroy themselves within. This is what happened in Rome. The real fact is do not expect much to change. The stronger (Anti God Crowd) will win out, until Christ returns. The strangling of American liberty is in affect and soon what we knew as liberty will be gone.

Vice President Dick Cheney made the following statement on April 8, 2015.. Former Vice President Dick Cheney on Tuesday floated one of the "theories" he's heard about Barack Obama — that the president may just be intentionally trying to destroy America from the inside.

Cheney sketched out the idea in an interview with rightwing radio host Hugh Hewitt.

[24] *"I vacillate between the various theories I've heard, but you know, if you had somebody as president who wanted to take America down, who wanted to fundamentally weaken our position in the world and reduce our capacity to influence events, turn our back on our allies and encourage our adversaries, it would look exactly like what Barack Obama's doing," Cheney said.*

The scenario Cheney described was similar to the plot of "The Manchurian Candidate," a novel and film that told a story of a brainwashed American politician used as a sleeper agent by communists seeking to "take America down."

"I think his actions are constituted in my mind those of the worst president we've ever had," the former vice president added.

As I look at it today, Obama has pushed that he is a Christian yet we see no proof in his decisions. I still stand on the fact he is a Muslim, and has hung out with Nation of Islam. The real problem is he understands the Arabic form of Islam and the Nation of Islam. He has and will continue to play both groups.

We do have an answer!

I have mentioned Biblical Liberty as quoted by the Bible, but we need to take another step. **Jeremiah 29:7 (KJV)** [7] And seek the peace of the city whither I have caused you to be carried away captives, and pray unto the LORD for it: for in the peace thereof shall ye have peace.

---

[24] http://talkingpointsmemo.com/livewire/dick-cheney-obama-take-america-down

We should make all efforts to seek peace and hold to God. If our Lord should tarry, the mission is still to reach people with the Gospel of Christ. We cannot go back and redo what has already happened however; we can start "praying today for God to change things." **1 Timothy 2:1-8 (KJV)** [1] I exhort therefore, that, first of all, supplications, prayers, intercessions, *and* giving of thanks, be made for all men;

[2] For kings, and *for* all that are in authority; that we may lead a quiet and peaceable life in all godliness and honesty.

[3] For this *is* good and acceptable in the sight of God our Saviour;

[4] Who will have all men to be saved, and to come unto the knowledge of the truth.

[5] For *there is* one God, and one mediator between God and men, the man Christ Jesus;

[6] Who gave himself a ransom for all, to be testified in due time.

[7] Whereunto I am ordained a preacher, and an apostle, (I speak the truth in Christ, *and* lie not;) a teacher of the Gentiles in faith and verity.

[8] I will therefore that men pray every where, lifting up holy hands, without wrath and doubting.

As a nation, we need to come back to prayer. In some of my meeting I always use the illustration, Muslims pray five times a day, just imagine what we as Christians could accomplish if we prayed five times a day.

Are You a Christian?

"For whoever will call on the name of the Lord will be saved."
- Romans 10:13

How You Can Know God's Love

"There is a God in Heaven who loves you as you are and not as you should be."

Yes... you are right... there is a God. You know that must be true. The heart of the human being longs for God, and logic demands divine existence.

While everyone believes, God is... most sense separation from God. We know God must be holy and good. We see ourselves as unholy and not good.

We conclude that God is angry with us and we cannot know Him.

Good News! This Testament of God's love is His Word to tell us that He loves us as we are. That love will save us from our sin and make us what we should be as God's children.

John 3:16
"For God so loved the world, that He gave His only begotten Son, that whoever believes in Him shall not perish, but have eternal life."

We hear Jesus say, "God so loved the world." God's love has no limitations.

He loves "so". More than we can imagine. He loves everyone - not just some ones.

Romans 5:8
 tells us that God loved us so that "when we were in our sin Christ Jesus came to die for us."

Romans 3:23

"for all have sinned and fall short of the glory of God,"
This verse tells us that all people have sinned. We have fallen short of God's intended purpose for us. God made us to know Him.... to receive His love and to love him in return.
For love to be love... for God to be God... and for humans to be humans.... God gave us a choice. We can choose to love ourselves and turn to our selfish pursuits. That is sin. In our sin we cannot know God and His love.
The result of sin is that we are lost... separated from God.

Romans 6:23
"For the wages of sin is death, but the free gift of God is eternal life in Christ Jesus our Lord."
Wages are just payment... due reward... what one has coming because of labor. The just payment for our sin is death.
Death here means spiritual insensitivity. When we are still in our sin, we have no life with God. We are alive physically but dead spiritually. If we continue in that condition, we will be separated from God for all eternity.
The wages of sin is death. but God's free gift is eternal life. While wages are earned, a gift is offered... no strings attached. God says He will give us eternal life - life with Him - in the place of sin's payment of death.
How can God remain true to His holiness and forgive unholy sinners? Because Jesus, His Son, has paid the price for sin by His death on the cross.

Second Corinthians 5:21 says, "He who knew no sin became sin for us, that we may be made the righteousness of God through Him."
Jesus arose from the grave to conquer sin and death for all who receive Him as God's free gift.

How can you receive God's free gift of love and life?

Romans 10:9-10

Strangling of American Liberty

"that if you confess with your mouth Jesus as Lord, and believe in your heart that God raised Him from the dead, you will be saved; for with the heart a person believes, resulting in righteousness, and with the mouth he confesses, resulting in salvation."

A person receives God's free gift of love and life by placing faith in Jesus Christ. To believe is simply to take God at His word. With our heart (whole believing) we believe that Jesus is God's Son who died for our sin on the cross and arose from the grave to live in us as Savior and Lord.

To believe in Jesus will result in confessing that faith with one's mouth.
Do you acknowledge that you are a sinner?

Do you believe by faith that Jesus, God's Son, died for your sin on the cross?

Will you now confess Him as your Savior and Lord?
Romans 10:13
"for Whoever will call on the name of the Lord will be saved."
This verse says that any person who will call upon the name of Jesus, the Lord, shall be saved.

To call means simply to ask in prayer. The verse does not require one to know more... do better... clean up one's life... or in any way try to add to what Jesus has done for us.
Will you now call upon Jesus to save you from your sin so that you can know God's love and forgiveness?

Pray like this: "Dear God, I confess that I am a sinner, and I am sorry. I need a Savior. I know I cannot save myself. I believe by faith that Jesus, your Son, died on the cross to be my Savior. I believe He arose from the grave to live as my Lord. I turn from my sin. I ask You, Lord Jesus, to forgive my sin and come into my heart. I trust you as my Savior and receive you as my Lord. Thank you, Jesus, for saving me."

When anyone calls on the Lord in this manner, that one is saved according to God's Word. If you pray a prayer of repentance and faith, you are saved. You have God's word on it.

If you have prayed this prayer to receive Christ as your Lord and Savoir, why not record your decision to follow Jesus as follows. Often times, a good place to write this would be inside the cover of your bible:

Believing by faith that God loves me and sent His Son, Jesus Christ, to die for my sin and arise from the grave to live in me, I, _____, do this day, _____, repent of my sin and accept Jesus Christ as my personal Lord and Savior. According to the promise of God in Romans 10:13, I have

If you have prayed this prayer please contact me at as I want to send you some material to help you in your growth in Christ.

Strangling of American Liberty
Biographical Sketch of Dr. David N. Smeltz

Dr. David N. Smeltz received Christ in October of 1969 at Immanuel Baptist Church in Ft. Lauderdale, Florida after returning home from Vietnam. As a decorated veteran and with the war raging and depression setting in from the loss of all his friends, he turned to a drunkenness life style. A young woman suggested Christ and invited him to church. Under the ministry of Ray Sadler, he accepted Christ as his Lord and Saviour. The young woman, Susan Odell of Wayland, Massachusetts became his wife in February 1970 and they began serving at the church where he served as a youth pastor while attending Broward Junior College. In 1973 while ministering as choir director of First Baptist Church, in Margate, Florida, he surrendered to the Gospel Ministry. In January of 1974, he, entered Lynchburg Baptist College in Lynchburg, Virginia and in 1978, he graduated. He started his first church in the fall of 1978 in Halifax, Va. and within the first year, the church grew from zero to over 125: He baptizing 68 individuals. Within two years, the church purchased ten acres of land, built a new sanctuary, and started a Christian School and day care.

In 1981, he assumed the pastorate at Fellowship Baptist Church in South Bend Indiana. Within four years, the church grew to a high attendance of over 700 on a special day. A Christian Day Care, a Christian School and Bible Institute were started. Pastor Smeltz applied with Anchor Theological Seminary in Texarkana, Arkansas and completed A Master degree in Theology in 1982. In October of 1985, he received his Doctorate of Divinity from Anchor Theological Seminary. He also attended Jay Adam's school of Counseling and graduated in 1983. He has pastored in

David N Smeltz

Sumner, Washington, New York City and Virginia. While earning these degrees he also earned his Master's in mechanical, plumbing, and electrical contracting.

In the past forty-two years, he has assisted in planting over thirty churches in America and foreign countries. Under his leadership, he has also re-established five churches. In 2001, he assumed the pastorate of Faith Baptist Church of Rustburg, Virginia and led the church until December of 2006 when he and his wife surrendered to a fourth quarter ministry of training national pastors.

In 2004, he was appointed Chaplain of the Vietnam Veterans of America, State of Virginia. He has had the privilege of speaking at national cemetery function, national meetings, and many conferences associated with veterans and veteran's organizations. God has presented him with an ability to communicate with veterans and those in distress. His passion has touched the hearts of the veterans and people around the world. His Military decorations include; Commendation Medal with V device for valor, Vietnamese- Cross of Gallantry Medal, Presidential Citation Medal and other medals associated with the Vietnam era.

Over the last forty-two years, he has ministered in over 1000 churches including ministries in Brazil, Indonesia, Philippines, South Korea, Germany, Ukraine, Russia, Guatemala, Vietnam and Cambodia.

His Word of Truth Ministries began in 1973 as an evangelistic ministry. In 1997, he began "Just a Daily Thought," an internet devotional ministry that has been converted to a book ministry that now reaches thousands through the internet. Under his leadership and guidance of the Holy Spirit, thousands have come to know Christ. He has published twenty-three books and many pamphlets.

In 2006 after ministering in Indonesia God burdened his heart to spread the truth to the Muslim people. "He has published four books on Islam and teaches on Islam in churches around the world." In 2008, he began teaching conferences on Islam in many churches here in the states and abroad.

In January of 2011 he published a book called "Identity Theft" This book compares Allah with Yahweh and Christ with Muhammad and answers the question is Allah the Islamic god the same God as Yahweh? All of the books he has published are on Amazon.com

He and his wife Susan serve as missionaries training national pastors. You can reach him through his web site www.drdavidsmeltz.org or www.hiswordoftruth.com

www.ingramcontent.com/pod-product-compliance
Lightning Source LLC
Chambersburg PA
CBHW070654290526
45790CB00001B/314